Saving Louisiana?

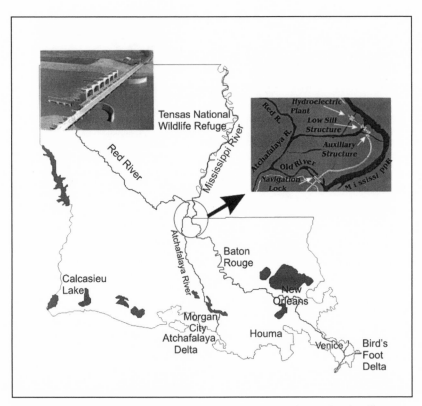

Map with some important features. Inset photograph shows the Auxiliary Control Structure at Old River.

Saving Louisiana?

THE BATTLE FOR COASTAL WETLANDS

Bill Streever

University Press of Mississippi
Jackson

http://www.upress.state.ms.us

The epigraph on page vi reprinted by permission of Oliver Sacks

09 08 07 06 05 04 03 02 01   4 3 2 1

Library of Congress Cataloging-in-Publication Data

Streever, Bill.
Saving Louisiana? the battle for coastal wetlands / Bill Streever.
        p.   cm.
Includes bibliographical references and index.
ISBN 1-57806-329-9 (cloth : alk. paper)—ISBN 1-57806-348-5 (pbk. : alk. paper)
1. Wetland restoration—Louisiana.   I. Title.

QH76.5.L8 S77   2001
333.91′8153′09763—dc21   2001026042

British Cataloging-in-Publication Data available

*To Ishmael Streever and Lucy
Slevin, whose generation may
live to see Louisiana saved*

Science sometimes sees itself as impersonal, as "pure thought," independent of its historical and human origins. It is often taught as if this were the case. But science is a human enterprise through and through, an organic, evolving, human growth, with sudden spurts and arrests, and strange deviations, too. It grows out of its past, but never outgrows it, any more than we outgrow our own childhood.

—Oliver Sacks, *Hidden Histories of Science*

CONTENTS

Acknowledgments   ix

The End of Deltaic Birth?   3

Multidimensional Thinking and the Louisiana Coast   18

Gaining Ground in the Atchafalaya   46

Watching the Marsh Sink   64

Educational Fishing   83

Good Business   100

Upriver   115

Living in the Bayou   134

Contaminated Paradise   154

Lessons from Louisiana   170

Notes   181

Index   187

ACKNOWLEDGMENTS

The enthusiasm, intelligence, and generosity of the many people inter-viewed for this book made my job, as a writer, tremendously enjoyable. Sam Faulkner, Jason Hale, Karen Johnson, Jim Slevin, Kristy Snedden, Louise Streever, and Kathy Temple provided helpful comments on draft chapters as well as encouragement. At the University Press of Mississippi, Craig Gill kept this book moving toward publication and distribution. Ima and Ishmael Streever were supportive throughout the eighteen months that it took to write *Saving Louisiana?* and they readily forgave me for spending far too many weekends and late nights in front of a computer screen.

Saving Louisiana?

The End of Deltaic Birth?

The Old River Control Structure, a series of steel gates mounted in the Mississippi River levee 170 miles upstream from New Orleans, very nearly failed in 1973. The map of America almost changed. If the structure had failed, the lower end of the Mississippi River would have swung to the west, following the course of the Atchafalaya River. Rather than flowing past Baton Rouge and New Orleans to discharge through the Bird's Foot Delta into deep Gulf of Mexico water, a distance of 315 miles, the longest river in North America would have discharged into the shallows of Atchafalaya Bay, only 142 miles away, down a steeper gradient to sea level. If the Old River Control Structure had failed, colossal flows would have moved down the Atchafalaya River, creating ten-story-deep scour holes that would have migrated along the riverbed, undermining bridge pilings. The Interstate 10 bridge would have collapsed. The U.S. Highway 190 bridge would have collapsed. Scouring would have exposed gas and oil pipelines buried beneath the bed of the Atchafalaya River, and, unsupported, they would have shivered in the flow and then, after some time, ruptured from the continuous stress. Gas supplies as far away as Massachusetts and Rhode Island would have been interrupted. Floodwaters would have isolated and then overcome Houma, Raceland, and Thibodaux. Morgan City would have been drowned, too, and then buried—

drowned by rising floodwaters and buried by silt as floodwaters receded. Rotting carcasses of drowned wildlife and livestock would have been snagged in tree branches and beached on high ground when water levels dropped.

After the flood, return to the status quo would not have been possible. With the Old River Control Structure washed out, most of the flow of the Mississippi River would have continued down the Atchafalaya River. At the Old River Control Structure, the Mississippi River's bed is below sea level, and, if the structure had failed, the reduced flow in the Mississippi River downstream from the structure would have been overcome by the pressure of saltwater from the Gulf of Mexico. A salt wedge would have extended upstream from the Gulf, underneath the lighter freshwater, contaminating water supplies needed for drinking and industry, first in Port Sulphur and then in New Orleans itself. Authorities would have had to truck in and ration drinking water. As salinities increased, power plants using river water for cooling would have had to shut down or face plumbing failure from saltwater corrosion. If municipalities continued to supply water for bathing and laundry, residential plumbing would corrode. Water heaters would be especially susceptible. Freshwater needed to process sugarcane no longer would have been available. The Mississippi River channel just south of the Old River Control Structure would have silted in, cutting off barge traffic, isolating the nation's seventh and fourth busiest port cities, New Orleans and Baton Rouge, from the barge routes north to Memphis, Saint Louis, and Minneapolis. The outlet of the Atchafalaya River, which allows ship traffic to move in and out of Morgan City, would have silted in. Oyster and shrimp fisheries would have crashed from changes in water quality.[1]

But the Old River Control Structure did not fail. Throughout the winter of 1972 and spring of 1973, the Old River Control Structure regulated the flow of repeated flood pulses tumbling down the Mississippi River, releasing some of the water into the Atchafalaya River, behind the structure, and thereby lowering the Mississippi River downstream from the structure, keeping flood waters from over-topping levees, protecting New Orleans and Baton Rouge from high water.

The structure had been designed for events as bad and worse than the flood of 1973. What caused the near failure? For the conditions existing when the structure was designed, it was more than adequate. But the rivers—both the Mississippi and the Atchafalaya—had changed since the structure was designed. The Mississippi River below the structure, toward New Orleans and the Gulf of Mexico, did not have the capacity that it had twenty years earlier. New levees contained its flow, held it in, pinched it. Changes to the watershed and the river itself changed the behavior of flood peaks. In 1940, a flow of 850,000 cubic feet per second resulted in a river height of just over 39 feet at Saint Louis, but the same flow in 1973 resulted in a river height of 43 feet. The 30 percent of the Mississippi River's water that was routinely released through the Old River Control Structure during periods of normal flow had deepened the Atchafalaya River. Water moved more quickly down the Atchafalaya than it had when the structure was designed. In 1973, at flood stage, the Old River Control Structure was only marginally adequate. Scouring in front of the Low Sill Structure—part of the Old River Control Structure—dug downward, exposing 50 feet of the steel pilings that supported the structure. A whirlpool formed. A 67-foot-tall concrete wing wall designed to guide flow through the structure's openings collapsed. The Old River Control Structure almost lost control.

Now, 50 rural two-lane highway miles north of Baton Rouge, Louisiana, 40 rural two-lane highway miles south of Natchez, Mississippi, surrounded by cotton and grazing land interspersed with swamp forest, I stand next to the repaired Low Sill Structure. It is late in the afternoon in January 1999. The stifling heat and soggy air of Louisiana summer are months away. The sky is deep blue and cloudless. The sun is shining. A light breeze blows.

Some distance away, at the upstream end of the canal that leads to the Low Sill Structure, the Mississippi River goes about its business, well below flood stage. During the year, if this is an average year, 145 cubic miles of water will flow past, enough water to fill more than twenty swimming pools for every man, woman, and child in the United States. In the same year, the river will carry 210 million tons of sediment to the Gulf of Mexico, an amount more than ten times the combined weight of every man, woman, and child in the United States. From the Low Sill Structure, it would be difficult to get down to the water, to touch the Mississippi River. The banks of the canal connecting the structure and the Mississippi River are steep and protected by fences. Piled stone, slick with mud and algae, supplements fences, stretching along the canal's edge, a fortified border between land and water.

In front of me but some distance away, beyond the massive pile of stone that replaced the 67-foot-tall collapsed wing wall, the water stain of higher river levels marks the tree trunks of a cypress forest. The trees are naked with winter leaflessness, and from here the water stain is a straight line several feet above the swollen bases of the trees, a subtle color change, little more than a shadow against gray bark. On the structure itself, a fading stain on the concrete, a scant 6 feet from the top of the structure, marks the 1997 high water. Behind me, across the road, water discharges through three partly open gates in the Low Sill Structure, dropping from the level of the Mississippi River to that of the Atchafalaya River. In all, there are eleven gates, each one 44 feet wide, each in its own concrete bay. After the water drops through the structure, it splashes up 12 feet against the structure's walls and forms standing waves 6 feet tall in the middle of the channel. It is flowing toward the Atchafalaya River, but not with the calm regularity of a slow southern stream. The surface is chaotic, a mixing bowl, white water foam contrasting against chocolate brown whirlpools and eddies. At the top of the structure a sign with white letters against a red background says "Danger Turbulent Water Keep 175 Feet Back." There is no punctuation and no threat of fines for violators. The water itself negates the need for punctuation and fines.

Back in my car, I drive across the structure, over the turbulence, a few minutes south. I stop at the Old River Control Structure office. The office is next to the Old River Auxiliary Control Structure, built after the near-disaster of 1973 to provide an alternative path of flow into the Atchafalaya, an extra safety valve for an overzealous Mississippi River. I want to talk to the workers, the men who control the structure that controls the Missis-

The Low Sill Structure, part of the Old River Control Structure. The sign near the middle of the structure says "Danger Turbulent Water Keep 175 Feet Back."

sippi River. The man I find in the office is perhaps thirty-five years old, with a southern accent, but not the accent of Louisiana. His waistline strains the fabric of too tight jeans, a sign that the battle to control the Mississippi River is fought from behind a desk. I tell him that I am interested in the flood of 1973.

"I'm from South Carolina," he tells me. "And I was just a boy in 1973. But I can tell you anything you want to know about the structure."

He has an uneasy smile that exposes beautifully straight white teeth and transforms itself into a nervous drawn-out clucking chuckle when I ask questions that he cannot answer. When I ask him how much concrete is in the structure, he clucks. When I ask him how they replaced the collapsed wing wall, he clucks again. When I ask him the thickness of the steel floodgates, he supplements his clucking with a fidgety dance, moving his weight from one foot to the other several times. He turns his lack of knowledge into a joke. "You stumped me again," he says, smiling, clucking, dancing. "I feel like I'm failing an exam." But when I ask him if he

7

knows anything about the impact of the Old River Control Structure on Louisiana's wetlands, he ends our conversation. "Our office of Counsel," he tells me, "has instructed us not to answer any questions about wetlands." He is still clucking, still dancing, but now he is very serious. He hands me a black-and-white brochure called "Atchafalaya Outlet Mississippi River and Tributaries," published in 1981.[2] Then he places one hand on my shoulder and walks me to the door. He tells me that I am welcome to look around on my own. Our conversation is over.

I drive farther south and park near the locks. There is a boat ramp in the parking area, and at the edge of the boat ramp I can touch the water. From a distance, at the Low Sill Structure, the water had the color of chocolate, but close up the color is more like creamed coffee. Suspended sediment in the water flows in loops and swirls. I let the water lap around the soles of my boots.

Next to the boat ramp, a man wearing a red ball cap low over his eyes sits in a van with his window down. Other than his van and my car, the parking lot next to the boat ramp is empty. He is a crew member on a tugboat, waiting for his boat. He will leave the van with the man he is replacing. The tug is coming down from the Black River, which joins with the Little River to become the Red River, which flows south to become the Atchafalaya River below the Old River Control Structure. Boats shuffle back and forth between the Mississippi River and the Atchafalaya-Red through the lock. The man does not know how long it takes to pass through the lock, or where his tug is going after it meets him. He is just crew, he tells me. His accent is from somewhere far to the north.

The lock exits into a canal before it joins the short stretch of water known as Old River, just below the Old River Control Structure, on the Atchafalaya River side of the structure. From there, Old River flows into the Atchafalaya-Red. In the fourteenth century, the Red flowed parallel to the Mississippi, but the two rivers did not join. By the seventeenth century, a bend in the Mississippi—a meandering loop of current later called Turnbull's Bend—intercepted the Red, and the Red became a tributary of the Mississippi. Just downstream, the Atchafalaya acted as a distributary stream, sucking Mississippi River water away from the lower end of Turnbull's Bend. In 1831, the steamboat captain Henry Shreve cut a channel through the base of the peninsula that formed Turnbull's Bend, providing a shortcut known as Shreve's Cutoff. Shreve's Cutoff, being shorter and therefore steeper than Turnbull's Bend, captured the main flow of the Mississippi River. The upper half of Turnbull's Bend, abandoned by the Mississippi River, silted in, but the midsection remained open, flushed by the Red River's flow into the Atchafalaya River. The trailing end of the lower half of Turnbull's Bend still joined the Atchafalaya and Mississippi Rivers; and, depending on water heights in the Mississippi, Red, and Atchafalaya Rivers, water could flow in either direction through this connection. The connection became known as Old River in reference to the fact that, prior to Shreeve, it had in fact been the River—the Mississippi River.[3]

But there is more to the shifting of the Mississippi River than minor changes like the swing of Turnbull's Bend, a swing that captured the Red River. The main channel of the Mississippi River has swung back and forth for thousands of years, like a great serpent gradually snaking across the land. Three thousand years ago, the lower end of the Mississippi River flowed farther north than its current path, closer to what would become Biloxi, Mississippi. As the river spilled into the Gulf of Mexico and spread across the shallows, the current velocity slowed, and sediment carried in the water dropped out, accumulating on the floor of the Gulf of Mexico to form the Saint Bernard Delta. Sand dropped out first, and lighter sediments dropped out as the water spread farther into the Gulf. Where sediment accumulation created exposed flats during times of low water, marsh plants took hold. The marsh plants contributed to the process of land building. The current velocity, already slowed as it encountered the Gulf of Mexico and spread over a wider area, was slowed even further as it ran through stems and leaves, and more sediment dropped out of the water column. Roots seized the sediments and held them in place. And as the plants grew, converting carbon dioxide and water to plant matter, they added more material to the growing land, in the form of roots and decaying leaves. The roots pushed elevations higher from below, and decaying leaves and stems built onto the elevation from above.

But even as the sediment accumulated, it sank under its own weight.

In the parlance of coastal Louisiana, it subsided. Weight from newly deposited sediments bore down on the older deposits, slowly squeezing the grains more closely together. It was a race, a contest between subsidence, which lowered the elevation, and the combination of sediment deposition and plant growth, which raised the elevation. As long as the Mississippi River's sediment load and plant growth outpaced subsidence, the Saint Bernard Delta continued to grow. But as the growing delta extended outward into the Gulf of Mexico, lengthening the distance river water had to travel before it reached sea level, it became less efficient than alternative pathways; the Mississippi River could find a shorter, steeper path to sea level. A few centuries after the birth of Christ, around the time of the fall of the Han Dynasty, the Mississippi River abandoned the Saint Bernard Delta, swinging well to the southwest, running past points on the landscape corresponding to today's Houma and Port Fourchon, to form the Lafourche Delta. In the abandoned Saint Bernard Delta, subsidence outpaced deposition. Plant growth alone could not produce enough material to keep up with subsidence; without the Mississippi River's sediment, the Saint Bernard Delta began to sink. As the marsh elevations decreased, periods of prolonged flooding increased. The marsh plants, with only a limited tolerance to continuous flooding, died. They no longer produced leaves and roots that could offset the rate of subsidence; and, as dead roots disappeared, decomposing back to the carbon dioxide and water from which they had come, their ability to stabilize sediments also disappeared. Erosion added to subsidence. The Saint Bernard Delta began to disappear at a faster rate.

While the Saint Bernard Delta began to disappear, the Lafourche Delta began to grow. But near the end of the Middle Ages, as Thomas Aquinas wrote the *Summa Theologiae* and Genghis Khan organized cavalry assaults, the Mississippi River shifted again, this time to its present course—a long time ago for a historian, but no more than the bat of a geologist's eyelash. The Bird's Foot Delta was born.[4] As it formed, modern civilization grew up around the Mississippi River. Henry Shreve dug Shreve's Cutoff through the Turnbull's Bend peninsula. Plantation owners and government agencies built levee systems to manage the river, to protect a growing population from flooding, and to improve navigation. As the approach to flood control became more sophisticated, people realized that what appeared to be a permanent fixture in the landscape was in fact not permanent at all. The river's course could change, not just by a few miles, but by more than a hundred miles. By the 1940s, members of the Mississippi River Commission were openly discussing the possibility of the Atchafalaya River capturing the Mississippi. By May 1951, a study undertaken by the Mississippi River Commission concluded that the Atchafalaya–Old River channel would capture the Mississippi River before 1980 unless a regulating structure was installed. Seven short months later, a meeting of scientists and engineers convened; their job was to predict the effect of a regulating structure on the Mississippi and Atchafalaya Rivers. One of these scientists was Professor Hans Einstein, son of Albert Einstein. Hans Einstein's reputation as a hydraulic engineer was built around theories of sediment transport in rivers. He argued that success of a regulating structure would require a means of guiding sediment into the Atchafalaya, to prevent ongoing deepening of the Atchafalaya. It had to be more than just a water control structure. Discussions wandered toward detailed points of science and arguments about theory, and the group had to be reminded of the practical issues at hand. At a follow-up meeting in 1952, in the presence of open acknowledgment that precise predictions about the fate of the Mississippi River were not possible, support for a structure at Old River grew.

Congress authorized construction of the Old River Control Project in 1955. Seven years and $67 million later, the structure was completed. With the structure in place, the cycle that built the Bird's Foot Delta would not end in the same way that it had ended for the Saint Bernard Delta and the Lafourche Delta. But still, the cycle would end. The Bird's Foot Delta now extended far out into the Gulf of Mexico, out to the edge of the continental shelf. Mississippi River sediment that had built the Bird's Foot Delta in the shallows of the Gulf of Mexico, on the edge of the continental shelf, was now discharging into deep water, tumbling down the continental slope. The Mississippi River was spewing its sediment load into the abyss. No new marshes were being built. The Old River Control Project had saved New Orleans and Baton Rouge, but it had broken the cycle of deltaic death and birth.

At the locks, a man wearing a hard hat and dark blue coveralls pulls up in a white government utility vehicle. He is in his fifties. He has come down to the locks during his afternoon break to savor the weather. His brother-in-law has a new boat, he tells me, with swivel seats and an eighty-horsepower Mercury motor; and the man and his brother-in-law are thinking of taking it out that afternoon, after his shift. We talk about the Old River Control Structure. The man has been part of the structure's maintenance crew for most of his adult life. I tell him about my conversation at the office, about the moratorium on discussions about wetlands.

"I don't know why he told you we can't talk about wetlands," the man says. "Some of these young guys working for the government, they're so worried about rules and regulations that they start to imagine new ones. We talk to people about wetlands all the time." For several minutes we talk about the river and its effect on Louisiana's wetlands. His job occasionally has him guiding school groups, and he has heard all about wetlands before. He offers to show me around. I follow him to the Auxiliary Control Structure and then walk behind him onto the structure itself. Stringy cobwebs cross the walkway, and the man uses his hard hat to sweep the webs away as we walk. "They build new webs every night," he tells me.

He was here in 1973. He felt the Low Sill Structure trembling. He felt the fear of near failure. He helped dump stone where the wing wall had collapsed. He worked here throughout the construction of the Auxiliary Control Structure. "Since then," he tells me, "We've had water higher than the '73 flood." He pats the handrail on the edge of the Auxiliary Control Structure, then gives a sweeping gesture that takes in the structure as a whole. "With the new structure," he says, "we've never had a hint of a problem."

He unlocks a door and I follow him up some steps, into the humid shadows of the structure itself. At the top of the steps, a machine-gray electric motor linked to gears that drive a cable spool stands like an altar.

From the cable spool, the cables run down into the heart of the structure to the floodgates themselves. Black machine grease covers the gear teeth and the cables, but the rest of the machinery is remarkably clean—no rust, no splattered grease stains, just thick coats of fresh gray paint over steel. "Each gate weighs a million pounds," the man tells me. "These motors only have forty horsepower, but with gear reduction that's all we need to lift the gates. We normally move them up and down one at a time, but with the emergency override we can move all of the gates up at once if we need to." On the control panel, there are five blue buttons and three red buttons. The three red buttons are labeled "raise," "lower," and "stop." An electronic meter with a red face is labeled "FEET OF OPENING." This is all it takes to control the Mississippi River: a few buttons, a small electric motor, and gear reduction.

He tells me about the Sidney A. Murray Hydroelectric Station, just upriver from the Low Sill Structure. "It uses the difference in water levels between the Mississippi and the Atchafalaya to generate power," he says. The power plant was built in New Orleans and towed upriver, the largest object ever floated past Baton Rouge. But the man thinks that claims of lower power rates resulting from the power plant are a lie. It cost $500 million to build, and someone is still paying for that, he asserts. And because a portion of the 30 percent of the Mississippi River's flow reaches the Atchafalaya River via the power station, there is less flow to keep the approach channels to the Low Sill Control Structure and the Auxiliary Control Structure clear, which means that the approach channels have to be dredged more frequently. "Someone is paying for that, too," he says.

I ask him about the Project Flood, the flood for which the Old River Control Structure is designed. By some accounts, the Project Flood is a one-in-thousand-year flood, meaning not that it will only occur once in one thousand years, but that there is a one-in-one-thousand chance of it occurring in any one year. In contrast, the flood of 1973 has been described as a one-in-twenty-five-year flood. The Project Flood will carry 2,720,000 cubic feet of water per second, enough water to put every living room, city street, driveway, and garage floor in New Orleans under 4 feet of water in less than three hours. Depending on whose numbers are believed, this is somewhat more water than that which flowed during the Great Flood of 1927, the worst flood since European settlement. The leveed banks of the lower Mississippi River can pass no more than about 1,250,000 cubic feet per second, less than half the flow from the Project Flood. The Bonnet Carre Spillway, which allows high flows to be dumped into Lake Pontchartrain just above New Orleans, could siphon off 250,000 cubic feet per second. The Morganza Floodway, between Baton Rouge and the Old River Control Structure, could siphon off another 600,000 cubic feet per second. This leaves 620,000 cubic feet per second for the Old River Control Structure.

"Things would get exciting around here," he says. "We would see some serious backwater flooding, up through the Red River. And the fuse plug levee at the West Atchafalaya Floodway would probably go. It's designed to go. I guess we'd see bad flooding all up and down the river. But the structure would be okay. It's overbuilt. It would be fine."

I remind the man that many people believe the structure will fail. From my notebook, I read a quote from a report produced by the Louisiana Water Resources Institute: "Probably the most important single conclusion reached by this study is that in the long run the Atchafalaya River will become the principal distributary of the Mississippi River and that the current main-stem will become an estuary of the Gulf of Mexico."[5]

"I've seen other reports that say the same thing," I add.

"You know," he says, "the people who write these things live off of government money. They need the government to give them money. They say things like that. They predict that the Old River Control Structure will fail. And they can't be ignored. They get some money, and they do some kind of study, and it usually costs more than they expected. But that doesn't mean they're right."

He stops, thinking about what he has said. "People worry about the Project Flood," he says. "I get questions about the Project Flood all the time. But I'll tell you something that no one asks about, that's terrorism." He pauses again, sweeping the area with his gaze as if looking for trouble—the control panel, the gears, the cables running down into the structure, the steps leading up from outside. Then, facing the control panel, he looks at me from the corner of his eyes. I cannot tell if I am a suspect, or if he is concerned about my impression of this odd statement. I say nothing, waiting for him to go on.

"Never mind the Project Flood. Say we get a one-in-twenty-five-year flood. Just a little higher than a typical spring water level. What's to stop someone from sabotaging the Old River Control Structure? It's a prime target. Destroying the Old River Control Structure at the right time, letting the Mississippi change course, would cause billions of dollars worth of damage. What happened in Oklahoma City would be nothing by comparison."

He pauses once more, looking right at me, almost certainly sizing up my opinion of his comment. "Like Clive Cussler's thriller," I suggest. "*Flood Tide*, wasn't it? Plant some explosives right here at the gates, or at the Low Sill Structure."

"Forget about that. The way to do it would be to take out the levee two miles upstream. The government itself has done the homework on blowing up levees. My nephew, he's a computer person. He pulled a government paper off the Internet. Laid out just how to do it. All it would take is a few pipes driven into the top of the levee to forty inches or so, then filled with blasting slurry. It would blow a small trench across the top of the levee. Once things got going, the water would do the rest of the work. It could happen. No one guards the levee. There could be explosives buried in the levee right now, and no one would know."

I follow him back down the stairs, out into the sun. We stand facing the Mississippi River, squinting while our eyes adjust. "I'll tell you something I hear all the time, something that annoys me. We get student groups through here—college students from New Orleans, mostly, and some from Baton Rouge, and others. Seems like everyone is interested in the Old River Control Structure. What gets me is that they come in here thinking they know everything there is to know. They think the Old River Control Structure is going to fail. They have some vision of the natural world overpowering the man-made world. They come in here and talk about arrogance and hubris. First time I heard the word 'hubris' was from a Tulane college student. I had to ask someone what it meant. You know what 'hubris' is?"

"Unreasonable over confidence," I suggest. "A god-like feeling."

"A god-like feeling," he nods. "That's it. But the fact is that this is just engineering. Just water held back by a dam. Not even a very high dam at that. And they want to know why we do it. They think we should let the river go. Let it follow its own way. They think that all the wetlands disappearing in Louisiana are because of the structure."

"Wetlands are good," I say. "People like wetlands."

"Wetlands are good," he says, his tone rising toward irritation. "Wetlands are great. Swamps and marshes both. That's what we used to call them, swamps and marshes. Now they're wetlands. I've been hunting and fishing as long as I remember, and no one likes wetlands more than I do. But Louisiana's wetlands aren't disappearing just because of the Old River Control Structure. Read the newspapers. We've got experts behind every tree—professors, government scientists. They all think they know what's gone wrong with Louisiana's wetlands. Trouble is, they can't agree with one another. You look at the facts, size everything up, and the picture is blurred. Maybe it's the Old River Control Structure, or maybe it's oil field canals, or maybe it's sea level rise, or who knows what else. And it's not just in the Delta that the wetlands are disappearing. Up and down the river the bottomlands are gone. And not just here. All along the Ouachita River, too. Take a ride along any river or bayou in Louisiana and you'll see the same thing. It's not the Old River Control Structure. At least, it's not just the Old River Control Structure. But people want something to blame. We've got this big structure right here. This big chunk of concrete and steel, out here in the middle of nowhere, run by the government. What a great thing to pin the blame on."

To our right, thirty feet from us, a great blue heron perches on the structure's handrail. We look at the bird. The bird looks at us. Its neck bends with the sinuosity of a river. With a jerking motion, as if startled by something that we cannot see, the bird turns its head away to look toward the Mississippi River. It lets forth a guttural squawk, then stretches its wings and hops off of the rail, falling downward to gain speed. Then, with a single slow flapping motion, it regains lost altitude. It squawks again.

I take the opportunity to explain that I am working on a book about Louisiana's wetland situation—about multimillion dollar spending on wetland restoration and the role of science in this process. I am looking for answers. Can we save Louisiana? Is it worth trying? What happens if we fail or if we walk away without trying? How are scientists contributing to the process?

The man leans against the rail, propped on his elbows, watching the heron, now almost invisible as it moves closer to the river. "The government is wrong most of the time," he says. "The government makes dumb mistakes. Vietnam. Watergate. Thousand-dollar hammers. This whole mess with Clinton's love life." He stands up straight, stepping back from the rail, then uses one hand to take off his hard hat before running the other hand through his hair, straight back across his skull, smoothing out wrinkles. "But here," he says, "the government is not wrong. I don't care what the scientists say. We can't let the Mississippi River change course. This structure is the right thing to do."

Multidimensional Thinking
and the Louisiana Coast

S ome people in Louisiana cannot talk about Gene Turner without swearing. A few people in Louisiana cannot talk about Gene Turner without swearing loudly. Here in his office, in an old metal-sheathed ex-military building on the Louisiana State University campus, this level of emotion is hard to fathom. Gene is fifty-four years old. His hair, in need of a trim, is graying and thinning. His mustache hangs past the corners of his mouth. Unruly dark eyebrows streaked with gray frame Gene's eyes. He wears leather hand braces to control carpal tunnel syndrome. While we talk, we are occasionally interrupted by students facing crises, by younger faculty members in need of quick advice and signatures, by secretaries offering cake and coffee. Gene sits with his back to a small wood-veneer desk. A computer covers most of the desk space, and what the computer does not cover is buried under scattered papers with handwritten notes. In places, the office ceiling is stained from water leakage. On the wall above Gene's desk, a framed photograph shows a Zen archer named Shibata Sensei, standing in snow, wearing what appears to be rough wool, but with one arm exposed to the cold. Gene himself has spent time studying Zen, in part to cultivate what he refers to as "awareness without attachment."

Gray and green metal filing cabinets and government surplus book-shelves cover most of the floor space. Among the hundreds of volumes on his shelves, there are two copies of *Wetland Restoration and Creation: The Status of the Science.* Marjory Stoneman Douglas's *River of Grass* is wedged between two more technical volumes, and farther along the shelf, enig-matic among the volumes on wetlands, is a copy of *Select List of British Parliamentary Papers, 1833–1899.* On top of a stack of government reports is a copy of *Distribution and Abundance of Fishes and Invertebrates in Gulf of Mexico Estuaries.* Slide carousels in boxes are stacked next to books. There are piles of green-covered issues of *Wetlands Ecology and Manage-ment,* a quarterly scientific journal that Gene edits. There are copies of an article from the journal *Nature,* with authorship shared between Gene and his wife, Nancy Rabalais, a respected scientist and former president of the Estuarine Research Federation.[6] The article is built around investigation of the Gulf of Mexico's dead zone, work suggesting that the problem of pollution from agricultural chemicals is more than a local or even a re-gional issue, that agricultural runoff into the Mississippi River, runoff which comes from a drainage basin covering over 40 percent of the lower forty-eight states, is changing the Gulf of Mexico. For their work on the dead zone, the two of them received a $250,000 cash award, which they plan to use for research support.

We have been discussing "Wetland Losses in the Northern Gulf of Mex-ico: Multiple Working Hypotheses," an article Gene published in 1997 in a scientific journal called *Estuaries.*[7] The ideas in this article are the most recent cause of the swearing associated with Gene's name around Loui-siana.

"If I wrote that article again," he says, "I would probably mellow the message."

The article is written in the flat style of scientific literature, in the dull prose of dissimulated objectivity. But his message is clear: wetland loss is not from sediment starvation and subsidence, not from controlling the Mississippi River, but from extensive coastal zone canal construction, mostly for support of the oil and gas industry. The canals change the way water moves across the landscape. It is the canals that allow subsidence to outpace accumulation of material, not changes to the river that block sediment flow.

The article starts with a key point: direct impacts to Louisiana wetlands have resulted in only about 12 percent of total losses. That is, digging of canals, along with intentional filling and draining of wetlands for agriculture and other purposes, has left a footprint that accounts for only 12 percent of the problem. The other 88 percent of losses occurs without direct, on-site human effort. Then the article goes on to test four hypotheses about the 88 percent of wetland losses occurring without direct, on-site impacts. Of the four hypotheses, three are cast aside. Two rejected hypotheses blame wetland loss on changes to the river—changes that prevent sediment carried in river water from flowing onto wetlands, leading to sediment starvation, which is the most widely accepted cause of wetland loss in the state. The other rejected hypothesis blames increased salinities and the ability of salt to kill plants in what were once freshwater wetlands. The surviving hypothesis blames canals. Gene tested the canal hypothesis with data from maps showing how the landscape changed over time. The relationship is simple—as the amount of land covered by canals increases, the amount of indirect wetland loss increases. In the end, the key point is this: Not only do the canals account for the 12 percent of wetland losses resulting directly from digging, they also account for the other 88 percent of losses. Canals, Gene believes, cause almost all of Louisiana's wetland losses. The canals alter the natural marsh hydrology. Wetland loss—what Gene calls indirect loss, to distinguish it from the digging of canals—starts with plant death and subsidence leading to formation of ponds. As the ponds become more abundant, the marsh takes on a fragmented appearance. It breaks up. In time, the land disappears altogether.

The repercussions of this are important. First, some of the large-scale wetland restoration efforts in Louisiana are driven by the assumption that sediment starvation is the major culprit in wetland loss, a hypothesis that Gene's article rejects. If sediment starvation causes wetland loss at all, the amount of loss that it accounts for is insignificant relative to the amount that can be attributed to canals. Second, net wetland loss rates, both direct and indirect, will approach zero with or without vigorous and expensive management, provided that more canal construction is not allowed to occur. Restoration efforts might reverse some of the losses that have already occurred, but if the goal is to stop further losses, they are not needed. Simply ending direct losses—stopping further construction of canals—will end indirect losses.

"I presented this information at a scientific conference in 1997," Gene tells me. "They weren't ready for it. Someone asked if I was joking. The president of the Louisiana Land and Exploration company called me a 'two-dimensional thinker' in a letter to the *Times-Picayune*. A 'two-dimensional thinker'—I couldn't believe it."

Later, wanting to find out what was meant by the phrase "two-dimensional thinker," I read the letter. Under a headline proclaiming "Off-base about wetlands loss," the letter says that Gene is wrong to associate most of Louisiana's wetland loss with canal construction, that "three- and four-dimensional scientists say these canals are responsible for about 10 percent of the problem," and that a two-dimensional thinker like Gene can only comprehend the water flow that he sees at the surface.[8] The letter from the president of the Louisiana Land and Exploration company—a company that has played a hand in digging more than one canal—implies that Gene's efforts are propaganda and laments Gene's ability, through his position as an academic, to teach these ideas to university students. The tone of the letter is one of stifled swearing.

I suggest to Gene that people are upset because they foresee liability claims against industry, because they foresee existing efforts at restoration being discredited, because they—speaking now for the scientists—foresee their own work being attacked.

"We're looking at a paradigm shift," he answers. There is no hesitation in his voice—this is something he has thought about before. "Scientific understanding of deltaic formation comes from work in Louisiana. Before 1900, there was a basic understanding that Louisiana marshes came from Mississippi River sediments. People knew that the river had changed course more than once, and that each time it changed course new marshes were created. People knew how deltas formed. They could see that marshes would disappear when sediment supplies were cut off. It seemed obvious that sediment was the key to marsh formation and disappearance. Then I come along with this new idea. I say that what is happening now is not the same as what has happened in the past. The pace is all wrong. The Mississippi River abandoned the Saint Bernard Delta about three thousand years ago. Now, 60 percent of the Saint Bernard Delta's wetlands are gone. That's about two one-hundredths of a percent per year. Today, Louisiana's wetlands are disappearing about twenty times faster than this. In some areas, loss rates are more than a hundred times faster than loss rates in the abandoned Saint Bernard Delta."

An area the size of Rhode Island has disappeared since the 1930s.

"I have a passage here, from your article," I say. "You wrote, 'The effects of extensive human-induced changes on this coast have apparently overwhelmed the causal linkages identified in a historical reconstructionist view of deltaic gain and loss.' "[9]

"Yes," Gene says. There is pleasure in his eyes, but I cannot tell if it is pleasure at being quoted or the pleasure of an interesting idea. "Exactly. Understanding what went on before we started digging canals is important. But understanding that canals have changed the rules is even more important. That's the paradigm shift. That's what people need to come to grips with."

"You know that this has frustrated some people. Some people think that you're ignoring certain issues in order to support a particular point of view. People claim that you selectively look at data." More specifically, some people think that Gene is out of step with the rest of Louisiana, that the article we are discussing should never have been published, that Gene is crazy. And then there is the swearing.

"Paradigm shifts always make people nervous. But paradigm shifts are what move science ahead."

Some years before, Gene had given me a book by a scientific philosopher named Paul Feyerabend.[10] Feyerabend's writings, which document historically important paradigm shifts, also point out that most of these shifts were only possible because of advocacy, including selective use of data, and that inconsistencies in the new paradigms were only corrected after the paradigm became widely accepted, when new data became available. "Feyerabend said that science moves forward because individual scientists have the backbone to advocate positions outside of the mainstream," I suggest. "Is it fair to say that what you are doing here is advocacy? Advocating a particular position?"

"Did Feyerabend call it advocacy?" Gene asks, smiling. He has a habit of breaking his conversation with short pauses, occasionally smoothing his mustache with thumb and forefinger, making it appear as though he is thinking carefully about his words. "I don't like to think of what I'm doing as advocacy. Not with the connotations that the word has taken on in recent times. But maybe it is, to the extent that I'm trying to make people open their minds. I just don't think that sediment starvation should be so blindly accepted. Other ideas should not be ignored. I may be wrong in what I'm saying about canals. But the possibility that canals are an important part of the puzzle should not be ignored."

"Do you feel as though you had to ignore certain data to put your point forward? Feyerabend believed that selective use of data was the norm in science." I am intentionally pushing Gene, looking for outward signs of irritation that would suggest personal involvement and loss of objectivity, but Gene is unmoved.

"I don't think I ignored any data." He pauses to run a thumb and forefinger down his mustache. "All I ignored was the old paradigm. I went into the problem without a preconceived answer. The answer that I came out with was not in line with the existing paradigm." Although he does not use the phrase, one might say that he had gone into the problem with a Zen foundation, aware but not attached.

During our conversation, he reminds me several times that he may be wrong, that part of being a scientist is the possibility of being wrong. It is important to keep an open mind, to know that one idea can be replaced by another. Twice in thirty minutes, he tells me that science should not be about personalities. Ideas should be attacked and dissected, and it is okay to be wrong. For the moment, he believes that the evidence supports his ideas, but he is open to other ways of thinking, if the evidence is there. It is clearly important to him that I understand this, that I recognize that he is not dogmatic.

Without solicitation from me, and without naming anyone, he comments on his detractors. "They argue that I'm wrong, but no one has come out with anything in writing—with a well-reasoned counterargument. And I've been through this before. I said once that diverting water into Lake Pontchartrain would cause algae blooms. Others said I was wrong, but when water was diverted algae growth took off. And now I'm involved with this dead-zone issue in the Gulf. But the data support the dead zone. The dead zone is real, and there's a clear trail linking it to the stuff coming down the Mississippi River." Various individuals and organizations, including some supported by fertilizer manufacturers, have attacked the dead-zone hypothesis. Undoubtedly, there has been more swearing.

I am in the cramped backseat of a twenty-year-old Cessna 180 floatplane, behind Gene. It has been several months since I last saw him, and he has grown a beard. Clay Perkins, our pilot, sits to Gene's left, wearing bright orange earplugs joined by a braided orange string that drapes behind his neck. Two thousand feet over Houma, in clear early morning skies, I look across the model-train landscape of south Louisiana. The metal sheds that characterize Louisiana oil-boom construction surround Houma's Intracoastal Waterway, but beyond the sheds are cane fields and swamp forests, one shade of green against another, giving way to a third shade of green—marsh—visible through the windshield, over Gene's left shoulder. In this part of Louisiana, people live in homes that hug the sides of roads, besieged on the only available high ground, if the phrase "high ground" can be invoked at all in south Louisiana.

The engine noise makes normal conversation impossible. On the ground, Clay had told us that he does not use intercom headsets in floatplanes because they create an entanglement risk if the plane goes down, and Gene and I are reduced to shouting back and forth. There is a great deal of pointing and lip reading. Intercoms would be convenient, but a floatplane is a necessity because we want to fly low, across as much of Louisiana's coastal zone as possible, which puts us a long way from anything resembling an emergency runway and a short distance from the ground. The point here is to see firsthand what photographs can only suggest: the extent of marsh loss associated with canal construction. But Gene also wants to show me how what he calls small restoration projects, which are typically ignored by big government programs, can contribute to the saving of Louisiana; and, importantly, he wants me to see backfilled canals, to understand that filling in disused canals can be a viable approach to restoration.

I ask Clay if he has seen the marsh break up over time, if the loss of marsh has been noticeable to him, as a pilot. "No doubt about it," he says. "It's obvious. It's horrible." It makes sense that he would notice, as a pilot, because he depends on the landscape to navigate. Losses mean more to him than numbers in a balance sheet.

Gene twists in his seat and says something, but the words are lost to the engine noise. I lean as far forward as my seat belt will allow, and Gene tries again, with one hand cupped around his mouth to form a megaphone. "Look at the difference between the canaled and uncanaled areas," he tells me. "Look at the open water around areas with canals and compare that to areas without canals." The difference is astonishing. Just below the plane, through the right window and down, the marsh, or what was once marsh, is little more than a maze of canals lined by banks of dredged sediment and surrounded by brown water. Ahead and to the left, through the pilot's window, an expanse of highly vegetated marsh, broken only by a twisting brown bayou, stretches toward the horizon to disappear in haze. It is as though I am looking at two different ecosystems: below me, something artificial, constructed, characterized by straight lines; ahead of me, wet wilderness.

The canals cross one another, dozens of straight lines of different widths, built for trapping, for pipelines, for access to oil wells, for navigation. Over six thousand miles of canals cut through Louisiana's coastal zone, scattered straight lines like pickup sticks strewn across the landscape. In the coastal zone, the area covered by canals roughly equals the amount of area covered by natural bayous—humans have doubled the amount of channelized flow through the Louisiana coastal zone. Blue floating boat barriers block the mouths of some canals. Scattered among the canals are oil wells and occasional boats. A small drill rig works at the end of one canal. Even from this altitude, I can see the spoil banks—the dredged material removed from the canals and piled along their edges. Many of the spoil banks are covered in trees or low shrubs, while the marsh itself, what little is left, supports only herbaceous vegetation; it is too low to support trees or shrubs. Immediately beyond the spoil banks, the canals are surrounded by shallow open water. Something like 90 percent of the vegetated area that I can see is on spoil banks. I know that this was once marsh, an unbroken expanse like the marsh ahead of the plane, but if I did not know the history of this landscape, it would be confusing. The eye focuses on the dark green spoil banks, and the mind thinks that this is a confused series of causeways, or someone's attempt to build lines of land, to make a gigantic canal estate that would offer every home a water view and water access.

Gene twists toward me, and I lean forward to listen. "The spoil banks last about sixty years," he shouts. "Sometimes they get thick with trees." He points forward, through the pilot's window, to the expanse of intact marsh. "In areas with fewer canals, the marsh is not breaking up as much. It's eroding, but it's a natural shoreline. There's some ditching, but it's much closer to being natural marsh." The ditches form straight streaks across the marsh, something that I had missed. They are abandoned ditches, only faintly visible, forgotten attempts to drain the land for agriculture and mosquito control.

Having climbed to two thousand feet, we fly at one hundred knots toward Head of Passes, near the mouth of the Mississippi River. Gene turns again, to point out the Delta Farms impoundment. When he turns, his elbow trips the door latch to the open position, but the wind keeps the door pinned. The impoundment, like other impoundments scattered through Louisiana's coastal zone, was built by enclosing large patches of ground with dikes, then draining the land within the dikes. The drained land is farmed. Many of the impoundments are relics of the Swamp Land Acts of the 1800s, acts which encouraged private developers to drain publicly owned wetlands. But draining marshland is not a one-time investment. Dikes require maintenance. Once the land is diked and drained, the soil is exposed to oxygen, and the organic component of the soil—that part of the soil comprised of decayed roots and stems—disappears, consumed by bacteria. The carbon that was so much of the soil becomes carbon dioxide. The surface within the impoundment, originally at the same elevation as the flooded land outside the impoundment, becomes deeper than the surrounding landscape. The pressure against the dikes grows. Dikes fail, especially during storms, and impoundments flood, forming deep lakes of open water where there had been marsh. The Delta Farms dikes failed in 1960. Now, Delta Farms is not a farm at all, but a roughly rectangular lake stretching across the landscape.

Gene tells me, over the engine noise, that the area north of Delta Farms had been diked and farmed in 1915. Some time after that, maybe after a hurricane, although he is not sure exactly when, the dikes had failed. Gene knows a man who, as a child, had helped drag a tractor out of the area. Now, the area north of Delta Farms has reverted entirely to marsh. In places, evidence of farming history remains: furrows and ditches are visible in the marsh. But nevertheless, it is marsh, self-restored, without a penny of taxpayer support. According to Gene, something like 1 percent of the marsh will recover each year if 10 percent of the dike is removed, whether the dike is removed by storms or by bulldozers. When he is done shouting he turns forward again. I reach forward and flip the door latch back to the closed position.

I track our progress on a map of Louisiana until I become lost somewhere over Barataria Bay. Where we are, my map shows no features, just green shading with little symbols shaped like multi-stemmed plants to indicate marsh and blue shading to indicate the open water of Barataria Bay. Off to the right, in the far distance, I can make out a string of light tan sandy beach at the edge of the Gulf. Just beyond the beach, in the Gulf, a shrimp boat leaves a trail of stirred-up sediment in its wake. But immediately to this side of the beach, the land, crisscrossed by canals, has subsided. Tiny green patches of marsh give way to coffee-colored water. There are permanent camps on stilts and scattered petroleum tanks. In places, the bottom is visible through what can be no more than a few inches of water, but there are also clouds of sediment, swirls of light-colored murk against the darker, deeper water of canals. Two parallel lines of dead trees mark the edges of a canal, illustrating a history of growth on spoil banks, followed by subsidence, followed by death from drowning. It occurs to me that the weight of the trees themselves may have increased the rate of subsidence and shortened the life of this spoil bank and its trees. I mention this to Gene, and he nods, but does not comment, leading me to believe that he may not have heard me or that my observation is too obvious to warrant comment. Already, my throat feels rough from shouting, and the temperature in the backseat is uncomfortably high. My shoulders and neck are cramped.

"Here's the trouble," Gene shouts. "Lots of sediment, but no marsh. Look at all of the sediment in the water, and there isn't any sign of marsh recovery. Too much of the marsh is gone. The wind crossing these long stretches of open water kicks up waves. It's just too much fetch for new marsh to develop. In triage, this would be a death. We would let it go and put our resources somewhere else. We would write this one off."

Below our right wing, the marsh is broken up. Dozens of canals cross the broken marsh. Gene, using aerial photographs and computers, has shown that ponds decrease in abundance as distance from canals increases. His data show that pond formation decreases to almost zero at a distance greater than two miles from a canal. I search for this pattern here, but there are too many canals. I see nothing that is more than two miles from a canal.

The radio's loudspeaker crackles in the plane's cabin, and Clay responds, holding a microphone close to his mouth—pilot talk, words lost to the engine noise. Venice, a town made up more of boats and floating oil field equipment than of homes, appears before us, at the end of Highway 23, an hour south of New Orleans by car, on the Mississippi River's western bank. With a certain landmark in sight, I look again at my map. We have traveled east and slightly south. By car, Venice is the end of the road moving down into the Bird's Foot Delta toward the Gulf of Mexico. But the land itself, if it can be called land, goes another twenty miles into the Gulf, splitting along the way into three long lobes that form a talon reaching out over the continental shelf. If conventional wisdom is right, the sediment discharging from the tips of that talon belongs in Louisiana and its exodus to deep water is the main culprit in wetland loss. If Gene is right, the 210 million tons of sediment discharging each year through the tips of the Bird's Foot Delta talon are not an important cause of wetland loss in Louisiana.

Clay, turning toward Gene and me, shouts, "Two minutes," holds up two fingers, and shouts again, "Two minutes." We are closing in on restoration sites in the Delta National Wildlife Refuge, a forty-eight-thousand-acre parcel owned by the federal government. Cubit's Gap, the subdelta on which the refuge is sited, was not here two hundred years ago. In 1862, soon after a woman known most commonly as "Cubit's daughter" had cut through the natural levees of the Mississippi River's east bank just south of Venice, floodwaters widened the ditch. Mississippi River water and sediments poured through, ultimately allowing something like two billion tons of sediment to bleed from the Mississippi River through Cubit's Gap, spreading into a fan-shaped lobe extending out from the Bird's Foot Delta, just above Pass a Loutre. By 1932, plants covered 90 percent of the new subdelta lobe. But over time, as the Cubit's Gap subdelta lobe reached out across Bay Rondo, its growth slowed, and then, from subsidence, it began to shrink. The smaller subdelta lobes rise and fall, following the same path as the full-scale delta lobes—the Bird's Foot; its predecessor, the Lafourche; and its predecessor, the Saint Bernard. But in the smaller delta lobes, the rise and fall pass more quickly. What might take more than a thousand years in a full-scale delta lobe happens in a century to a subdelta lobe. From 1956 to 1978, the wetlands that formed as the result of Cubit's daughter's propensity for digging declined by almost seventeen thousand acres, more than one square mile each year. The loss rate, if Gene's ideas are right, was accelerated by the presence of canals.

But in 1978, high water broke through levees that had formed along channels within the Cubit's Gap subdelta. Smaller subdeltas formed within Cubit's Gap subdelta. As marsh disappeared throughout most of Cubit's Gap subdelta, new marsh formed in these smaller subdeltas. New marshes form as splays, first fans of sediment finding their way through the breached levees, then mudflats, then vegetated wetlands. As splays

29

grow, they form landmasses that block the flow of water from the river. As a splay ages, the channels running through it divide, then divide again, leaving a series of bifurcations in the search for hydraulically efficient routes to sea level. Eventually, the routes through the splay become less efficient than the route down the main channel, and flow abandons the splay, leaving the subdelta to decline. But for a time, marsh grows, offsetting the overall decline in the larger Cubit's Gap subdelta, and offsetting, in a small way, the overall decline in the Bird's Foot Delta itself. This is Louisiana, growing and shrinking simultaneously, with new land here displacing lost land over there, a balance that has somehow swung out of balance so that now the new land cannot keep up with the lost land, over a million acres gone since 1930.

Gene opens a notebook of aerial photographs and looks alternately at the notebook and the landscape below the plane. We drop quickly, then level out at one thousand feet. Clay throttles back and starts a wide circle around a coordinate on a map, the location of an intentionally created break in the levee within the Cubit's Gap subdelta lobe. The idea is to duplicate the effects of nature. Where nature would breach the levees with high water, engineers can breach the levees with a floating dragline—a barge-mounted crane with a clam bucket replacing the hook at the end of its boom. It is the same kind of equipment used to dig many of the canals that have caused Gene to be called a two-dimensional thinker. Gene continues to alternate between the notebook and the landscape until I start to think that the coordinates may be wrong, but then he sees the match between photographs and landscape. He points. We circle the small crevasse that lets water and sediment flow from the main channel to the open water behind it, the open water that had been wetlands, for a while, before it had broken up and disappeared in the loss and gain of deltaic life.

"Looks pretty good," Gene shouts. Once located, it is easy to see. There is an obvious splay, a green fan reaching out from the breached levee into brown shallow water. Gene unlatches the window and eases it open on its hinges until the wind pins it against the bottom of the wing, then leans out to snap photographs of the site. Air rushes through the plane, drowning the engine noise. In the backseat, the wind flushes out the heat. With my own camera, I lean forward to snap shots through the open window. It is difficult to tell what is actually happening on the ground. The green has the brightness and tone of floating duckweed, perhaps taking advantage of the freshwater and nutrients of the river spilling out into the quiescent shallows beyond the levee. But it may be thick mats of anchored plants, a more permanent addition of land on the water. Or this spot may be in transition, on the verge of becoming shallow enough to support thick mats of anchored plants. From this altitude, it is unclear.

A crevasse splay. The canal at lower right is connected to the Mississippi River and the fan-shaped splay is newly forming wetland.

There is another crevasse a few minutes away, and another, and another. Between 1983 and 1995, the Delta National Wildlife Refuge, with the help of oil companies, the Corps of Engineers, and the U.S. Fish and Wildlife Service, created twenty-four crevasses. Below us now, a dragline works beside a levee, apparently digging a new crevasse. Nearby, new earth—bare brown against the thick green of undisturbed levee banks—marks a spot where the levee had been broken and repaired, apparently a mistaken crevasse, patched after it had been built. We drop to five hundred feet to look at a crevasse built almost a decade ago, but within sight of the dragline. The splay extending out from the crevasse looks as though it is covered with pickerelweed, a deeper green than duckweed. Pickerel-weed usually grows with its roots firmly anchored in soil. The glare of sunlight against water reflects up through the foliage. The crevasse splay has already become a miniature delta lobe, with a sinuous channel running through it and splitting several times before disappearing into the shallows of the bay. "This one has filled in well," Gene shouts, now having to overcome the wind and engine noise combined. He shoots more pictures.

Draglines cut the crevasses at a sixty-degree angle to the channel flow line, with a width of about one hundred feet and a length of one thousand feet.[11] Plans call for channels that slope upwards from the main channel, which is well below sea level, to the bay bottom; but, in fact, channels have to be deep enough to float construction barges, which means that long stretches of the crevasse channels are flat. Planners look for sites where open water encroaches close to the levee, to minimize length requirements for crevasse channels. Open water areas have to be bigger than about 140 acres for the effort to be worthwhile, and there must be an outlet channel running away from the open water, to provide a path for water flow. For twenty sites examined in 1995, wetland gain was just over 700 acres, or about 3 percent of the area lost per year for Louisiana, or about 4 percent of what the Delta National Wildlife Refuge lost between 1956 and 1978.[12] At average growth rates of about 12 acres per year, sixty-three crevasses would offset wetland losses in the Delta National Wildlife Refuge. But the splays, like natural delta lobes, do not grow at a constant rate, and averages are misleading. Crevasse splays may not grow at all in the first year, but in the fifth year they may grow more quickly than the average. Digging crevasses does not give an instant return.

Now we stay low, flying at five hundred feet. A yellow helicopter crosses our path, perhaps a mile away and one hundred feet above us. The wind from the window makes it difficult to take notes. Gene passes me an aerial photograph taken in 1995. The landscape has changed since then. Below the plane, at the end of a crevasse, the new marsh of a crevasse splay, shaped like a pie slice, stands out. In the photograph, only the crevasse is visible. In five years, the splay has developed. From this low altitude, the vegetation stands out: mats of duckweed, pale purple flowers of pickerel-weed, floating water lilies. Pelicans forage in groups, and nearby an egret struts through shallower water with its neck stretched out in search of prey. Gene closes the window, and without the wind I can hear my ears ringing.

Clay turns toward Gene and shouts, then looks at me. I point toward my ears and shrug, and he repeats himself. "I always wondered what the red stuff is," he says, referring to the streaks of brick red vegetation in the water, mixed with the duckweed.

"Azolla," I shout back. "Water fern. It's a floating plant. Small stuff. Just a little bigger than duckweed." My throat, by now, has made the transition from rough to scratchy. I feel increasingly nauseated; the vibration of air from the open window, the banking, the note-taking, the matching of aerials to the landscape, and now, with the window closed, the heat—it all combines to work on my stomach. Out past the marsh, near the horizon, offshore oil-field structures are visible. For a time, I focus on the structures, trying to control the motion sickness. Gene continues to take notes.

We climb and head west and north, back over the Mississippi River. A freighter with an orange superstructure and a black hull floats against the brown water of the Mississippi River's main channel. At one thousand feet, a helicopter passes below us, headed toward the Gulf. Over Venice, I notice a drill rig that I had not seen before. We pass a farmed impoundment, orange groves surrounded by marsh and protected by levees. There are more tank farms, mixed white tanks and older, rusting multi-colored tanks, with a barge moored nearby, taking on or discharging petroleum.

Gene turns back toward me, tripping the door latch again. "Every one of the crevasse sites is building," he says. Clearly, he is excited. "This looks good. Things have happened since '95." I nod, and when he turns forward I push the latch back to the closed position.

Gene's excitement interests me. The success of the crevasses seems to contradict Gene's belief in canals as culprits. Here, digging canals across natural river levees increases wetland area. But these are special canals, designed for wetland restoration, not for navigation or pipeline right-of-ways. And, in fact, what looks at first like a contradiction is not a contradiction at all. Gene thinks that canals are the primary culprit, far outweighing other causes of loss, but this does not rule out crevasses as a restoration tool. They can build land even if they cannot completely counteract the damage caused by the main culprit. But Gene's excitement interests me in another way. He has flown over Louisiana's coastal zone many times, and now his mind emphasizes the gains that he sees. This is my first flight over Louisiana's coastal zone. I see the gains, but what weighs heaviest on my mind are losses—hundreds of canals crossing one another at odd angles, subsiding marsh, dead trees, expanses of open water where there had once been wetlands. The crevasse splays are so small that they are hard to find on this broken landscape. They are Band-Aids for cancer.

While Clay refuels the plane, Gene and I stand next to the Intracoastal Waterway in Houma, simultaneously stretching muscles cramped by the too small seats of the floatplane and eating sandwiches. We talk about crevasse splays. Then Gene tells me about angry letters he has received and about letters sent to the university. At one point, although tenure offered substantial protection, he worried about losing his job. I suggest to him that he could interpret this reaction as a compliment: if they thought he was crazy, they would not feel threatened.

Money catalyzes some of the antagonism toward Gene and his ideas. The Coastal Wetland Protection, Planning, and Restoration Act calls for big spending: $33 million to $44 million a year for the past eight years, directly from the federal government, plus a variable number of nonfederal dollars from other sources. The bill is sometimes called the Breaux Bill, after its original backer in Congress, but it is more often known by its initials, as CWPPRA, usually run into the two-syllable pronunciation "cwip-ra." One projection calls for total spending from CWPPRA and associated programs—most of which are not currently funded—of something like $14 billion over the next three decades. This is, to the say the least, a considerable sum of money. Fourteen billion dollars worth of twenty-dollar bills, laid end to end, would stretch from New Orleans to

Washington, D.C., and back more than fifty times. It is $52 and change for every man, woman, and child in the United States, or over $3,000 a piece for Louisiana residents.

The money will go to different efforts. By 1999, eighty-one separate projects had been approved, and construction had been completed in more than a third of these projects. There are terraces, sediment traps, siphons, plantings, crevasses, piles of dredged material—all attempts to restore lost wetlands and protect those that remain. But $14 billion, in the context of an effort this big, tackling land loss equivalent in size to the entire state of Rhode Island and spread thinly across Louisiana's coastal zone, looks less impressive.

Money has become, in recent times, one of the themes of Gene's research, a place that his research has carried him. We talk about the cost of crevasse splays. If only young sites are assessed, the process looks expensive. Engineering and construction for three splays completed in 1992 cost $95,000 and yielded 33 acres by 1995, at a cost of $2,800 per acre. But as the sites continue to grow, costs per acre decrease. For the eight crevasse sites built between 1983 and 1987, costs were $140,000, and by 1995 these sites could be credited with 670 acres of wetland gain, for an average cost to taxpayers of just over $200 an acre. Over 10 years, an acre of wetland could be created for about the same cost as two hours of floatplane time. If all of the ponded areas below the crevasses filled in, the final cost would be less than $20 an acre. But there is an unknown here: no one knows how long the crevasses will build wetlands. Like natural deltas and subdeltas, the crevasse splays will go through a period of growth followed by decline. Best guesses suggest life spans between 50 and 150 years. If the rate of wetland gain stayed, on average, at 12 acres per year, complete recovery of wetlands in the ponded areas below crevasses would require 92 years. But rates of wetland gain will change over time; and eventually, splays created by breaching levees will begin to disappear. And this is one of the inescapable lessons of Louisiana: nothing is permanent. What comes also goes. Restoration contributes to a dynamic process, but it is an ongoing battle, an ongoing responsibility.

"Big projects are more expensive," Gene says. "CWPPRA likes big projects." According to Gene—and he has data to back up his thoughts—cost per acre goes up as total project cost goes up.[13] This is the antithesis of economy of scale. In the first four years of CWPPRA, only one project out of sixty-three cost less than $500,000. Big projects require expenditures for flood protection and other measures that do not contribute to wetland gains. Gene's numbers suggest that CWPPRA projects cost about $12,000 per acre of wetland—six hundred times more than the estimated cost per acre for crevasse splays. Gene has estimates for other approaches to restoration. Restoring abandoned impoundments by bulldozing levees costs somewhere between $25 and $100 per acre. Terracing, a method of dividing areas of open water into quiescent cells where sediments can settle out to build marsh, costs between $1,000 and $3,000 per acre. Back-filling canals costs less than $1,000 per acre. And spoil-bank management—reengineering the piles of material dredged from canals and haphazardly piled around Louisiana's coastal zone to form a vast network of unplanned dikes—could lead to restoration costs of less than $1 per acre, potentially twenty-thousand times less expensive than some CWPPRA projects. Even using CWPPRA's Wetland Value Assessment method, which accounts for decreased wetland loss rates as well as actual wetland gains, there is no economy of scale. The implied suggestion of waste adds one more reason for swearing about Gene.

"And big projects mean big failures," Gene says. "If you put all of your money in one project and it doesn't work, all that money is gone. If you divide your money between lots of small projects, and some fail while others succeed, you have made progress." In a 1994 article, hidden in the fine print of a six-hundred-word table, Gene alluded to this principle with the phrase "strength through diversity."[14]

After lunch, we head south and west, looking for backfilled canals. It is hotter now, and my nausea, which had all but disappeared on solid ground, is back. But I am staring out the window, looking at Louisiana. Somewhere out here, in these broken marshes, are opportunities for restoration: dozens of abandoned impoundments, hundreds of potential crevasse splays, thousands of canals that could be filled. Clay turns to me to trace our route on my map. For a moment, while he looks at the map, he lets the plane fly itself, no handed. We are approaching Morgan City, near the would-be course of the Mississippi River, were it not for the Old River Control Structure. The E. Donner gas field is below us, next to the Terrebonne-Lafourche drainage canal. Through a canopy of cypress trees, I can see duckweed floating on water. We move along the coast north of the main Atchafalaya River discharge into the Atchafalaya Delta, but we pass within sight of the outlet of Wax Lake, where part of the Atchafalaya's discharge finds it way to the Gulf. Like many of Louisiana's lakes, Wax Lake is really more of a bay than a lake. Below, I see new wetlands, a new delta forming at the mouth of the outlet on sediment transported down the Atchafalaya River. The water over Vermillion Bay is glass calm and only slightly too brown for pea soup, but considerably closer in color to pea soup than lentil soup. There are scattered wellheads, steel tripod platforms with valves that control the flow of petroleum, larger four-legged platforms with helicopter landing pads and machinery. Along shore, dead trees and stumps mark a sinking shoreline. A swamped shrimp boat lays abandoned and decaying in shallow water.

We pass over long stretches of the Intracoastal Waterway separated from the Gulf of Mexico by narrow bands of marsh. Sometime soon, certainly within my lifetime, these narrow bands will disappear and barges on the Intracoastal Waterway will have to contend with the wind and waves of full Gulf exposure.

Gene points out a backfilled canal, one of thirty-one that he has followed over time.[15] Clay descends and banks, and Gene opens his window to shoot pictures. The canal is backfilled, but it is still a canal—a straight line across the marsh, with the higher ground of spoil banks on both sides. "Backfilling success really depends on the dragline operator," Gene shouts. "He left big pieces of the spoil bank intact here. You can still see the trees growing." When canals are backfilled, there is seldom sufficient sediment to completely fill the canal, even with skilled dragline operators who do not leave parts of the spoil bank behind. After the canal is dug, the spoil banks sit for some time. The sediment dredged from the canal and piled alongside to become spoil banks dewaters, and as it loses water

A backfilled canal. Trees still grow on what remains of the spoil banks along the edge of the canal, but wetland vegetation is filling in the canal itself.

it shrinks. And the soil oxidizes, losing its organic component to bacteria, shrinking further, just as the soil of drained impoundments shrinks. On this canal, more material could have been scraped away from the spoil banks, but it still would not have completely filled the canal. This reduction in volume has led some to believe that backfilling is futile as a restoration method. "Backfilling starts the process," Gene shouts. "Once the spoil banks are lowered, marsh fills in from the edges." He has to repeat himself twice for me to understand.

We buzz backfilled canals every few minutes, one after another after another. Some look the same as unfilled canals. Others, completely grown over with vegetation, are hard to find against the background of marsh. We locate sites by comparing the surrounding landscape to Gene's five-year-old aerials. One that had been backfilled has been redredged. "Men undoing what men had undone," I shout to Gene, but he does not seem to hear, and I let it go. Heat and nausea make shouting too hard. I conserve my energy to look at canals.

Every canal is different, every situation is unique. For the thirty-three canals that Gene has tracked, lengths range from less than four hundred feet to more than a mile and areas range from just over one acre to just under four acres. Every canal restoration is different: the soil has different characteristics, the vegetation is different, the tidal regime is different. One point of looking at thirty-three canals is to search for patterns. And there are patterns. Backfilling is more effective in canals less than five years old, where substantial spoil banks remain and provide a source of material. Backfilling is more effective if surrounding marsh has low organic levels because spoil bank volume will not be as reduced by oxidation. Substantial gains in marsh area result from bringing spoil banks down to the elevation of the marsh, but less substantial gains result in the canals themselves, which remain too deep to support vegetation even after backfilling. But partly filling canals improves habitat. Submerged vegetation grows more often in the shallower depths of backfilled canals than in intact canals, and the backfilled canals support about six times the number of fish and invertebrates that intact canals support. Importantly, the number of individual animals that live in backfilled canals seems to be controlled by predation, while the number of animals living in intact canals seems to be controlled by the harsh physical conditions created by deep, still water. In short, the backfilled canals act more like natural marsh ponds and channels.

We have eased out of the Deltaic Plain and into airspace above the Chenier Plain, the western half of Louisiana's coastal zone. I know this because of marks on my map—the landscape itself does not change suddenly. On the Deltaic Plain, we had looked at twenty-four backfilled canals. "Almost all of them are filling in," Gene shouts back to me. Backfilled canals that he had seen several years before, where marsh development had been minimal, now have more marsh. Because Chenier Plain marshes have higher mineral content and lower organic carbon content than Deltaic Plain marshes, their spoil banks will not have oxidized away as quickly as those of the Deltaic Plain. Canals here on the Chenier Plain should be more suitable for backfilling than canals on the Deltaic Plain. We look at sites with names like Pecan Island East, Pecan Island West, and Mallard Bay East. But like the crevasse splays, restoration of canals takes time. Individually, through the floatplane's window, differences between Chenier Plain and Deltatic Plain backfilled canals are hard to spot. Information has to be converted to data, and data have to be compared to see the differences.

The canals we look at can only explain 12 percent of marsh loss in Louisiana. According to Gene, 88 percent of marsh loss comes from the indirect effect of canals, and the backfilling we see only accounts for direct losses. Because the backfilled canals are isolated cases, one here and one there scattered among intact canals, indirect losses may not be reversed. For backfilling to reverse indirect losses, if Gene is right, all of the canals in a large area would have to be backfilled, rather than individual canals. Many of the canals are still in use by landowners or leaseholders who need boat access to sites, making large-scale backfilling an unlikely proposition. But Gene has calculated that something like $500 million dollars would cover construction costs for backfilling all canals in the state, based on an estimated cost of $85,000 per mile of canal. Planning and legal costs would be a significant multiplier, but, nevertheless, the cost of filling most canals in Louisiana may be cheaper than the overall CWPPRA approach and, if Gene is right, filling canals could reverse wetland loss. Gene knows that filling all canals will not be possible, but what dismays him is that CWPPRA does not recognize backfilling as even a bit player in the future of Louisiana. My impression is that he sometimes has to work hard to resist the temptation to swear about CWPPRA's lack of interest in backfilling canals.

Off to the right, a dragline piles bay-bottom sediments into long lines of spoil. "Looks like a terrace," I shout to Gene. The idea here is to build a complex of long, low mounds, just high enough to reach above low tide. Wetland plants will grow on the mounds. Because the mounds will break up the wave action, sediment suspended in the water will fall out and accumulate in this newly protected environment. In a best case scenario, the sediment will build up the elevation of the surrounding shallows until plants take hold. It strikes me that there is something in common here with the abandoned agricultural impoundments that Gene had pointed out earlier. The mounds resemble the walls of small impoundments, breached at irregular intervals. Clay flies a tight circle around the dragline, clockwise, so that we are banked hard to the right. My weight rides on my right shoulder, leaning against the bulkhead. Gene, who has been flipping through his notes, turns to me and once again bumps open the door latch with his elbow, but again the wind holds the door in place and, as if our actions have become ritualized, I reach forward to reengage the latch.

"I don't have anything about this site," Gene shouts. The fact that Gene, as in touch with Louisiana restoration efforts as he is, knows nothing about this site suggests that, in all likelihood, no one has a handle on the full picture. Free enterprise has taken over. People try different things in different places, with money from different sources, finding to some degree what Gene himself called strength through diversity. It occurs to me, too, that there is a certain amount of irony down there in the marsh: for crevasse splays, canals breach levees to restore wetlands, but not far away, canals are filled to restore wetlands, or levees are built in the purposeful patterns of terraces to restore wetlands. Just past the dragline, the silhouette of a great blue heron glides next to the floatplane's shadow on the water, and a patch of water lilies grows, the white-against-green of water lily flowers over floating leaves.

We head west again, toward Texas. Straight ahead, a dark cloud stands up over the marsh, a towering cumulonimbus with thick rain underneath and occasional flashes of lightning, some running through the cloud itself and toward the ground. The cloud blocks the sun, but the sun's rays shine from behind the cloud in all directions. Immediately under the cloud, the ground is invisible, obscured by rain, but around the edges of the rain the ground reappears, blurred at first and then more clear, a mosaic of greens and browns. Clay banks gently to the right and gains altitude to avoid the storm. "Tighten your seat belts," he says, and as the plane turns the storm appears through the port window, still some distance away, but filling the entire view.

Somewhere past White Lake, we dip low to look at the Grand Lac L'Huit backfilled canal. It is fifteen hundred feet long and covers three and one-half acres. It was backfilled when it was eighteen years old, but before then its spoil banks covered an additional seven acres. Though the

Terraces at Calcasieu Lake

backfilled canal is still clearly discernible, it has filled in and become more marsh-like. By my count, it is the twenty-fifth canal that we have looked at today. We buzz three more canals, then skirt the western shoreline of Calcasieu Lake, looking for terraces built in the Sabine National Wildlife Refuge. The lake stretches more than 20 miles from north to south, and there is some confusion about the location of the terraces. When we find them, Clay banks to circle around them so that we can shoot photographs, then heads east, back toward Houma, 150 miles away. We climb to two thousand feet.

"That's what it should look like," Gene shouts. Below, tidal creeks of different widths meander across the marsh, with scattered small ponds surrounded by dense vegetation. A barrier beach stretches along the edge of the marsh, and behind it the Gulf of Mexico reaches out to the horizon. For a period of perhaps two minutes—a distance of maybe three miles—we fly over the old Louisiana, with intact marsh and only scattered canals. Then we are back over a broken landscape, interlaced by canals and crossed by roads, with large expanses of brown open water that were once, not long ago, marsh.

. . .

The following morning, back in Gene's office, Gene talks about his work. He sits with his back to his computer. The leather braces that control carpal tunnel syndrome encase his hands. I am in a broken chair; if I lean back, I will fall over. I have asked him, point blank, about the swearing associated with his name. He responds by comparing society and nature. "Society works by consensus. It is political and economic. There is a common will that moves things forward. But nature doesn't work that way. A biopolitical approach to restoration won't work. Nature doesn't care about human consensus." He suggests that the standing nail will be hammered down, and, more vividly, that politicians can eat scientists. Here, I think he means both professional and nonprofessional politicians—the players of academic politics.

"Science is competition for ideas," he says, making me think again of Feyerabend's writings about advocacy in science, but that is not what Gene is thinking of now. "Some ideas catch on and influence management. Twenty years ago, managers said that shrimp live in water and that replacement of marsh by open water would not hurt the shrimp industry. No one would say that now. And not long ago no one took the idea of indirect marsh loss as a consequence of canals very seriously. Now we argue about how much of the total marsh loss is caused by indirect effects of canals, but no one doubts that canals play some role."

I ask Gene about differences between what he sees going on in Louisiana and what he sees elsewhere—in the Florida Everglades, in the Chesapeake Bay, in the Puget Sound. "There's more money for science in other projects," he says. "And everyone else talks about hydrology, while we talk about sediments." This leads him naturally into discussion of spoil-bank management. In some ways, canal backfilling and breaching of levees around agricultural impoundments are forms of spoil-bank management. "Throughout Louisiana," he says, "natural hydrological processes have been interrupted. Flows have been blocked by canal spoil banks, by impoundments, by roads. Marshes rely on a balance of flooding and draining. If a spoil bank holds water on the marsh, soil conditions change and the marsh plants die. If a spoil bank blocks flow from the marsh, the organic component of the soil oxidizes and disappears, in essence consumed by bacteria." Marshes can only survive if there is a balance between flooding and draining—enough draining to keep the plants alive, enough flooding to prevent oxidation of soils.

"The spoil banks also block the flow of sediments," Gene adds. "There is something to that. But the main problem is hydrology. Louisiana marshes are living ecosystems, not just sediment."

While we talk, he pulls up information on his computer, data to support the conversation. He occasionally pauses to retrieve a reprinted publication from a file drawer or a bookshelf, and over twenty minutes I accumulate nine articles reprinted from scientific journals. One of them talks about the "volumetric leverage" of plant fiber in soils. A five-meter-deep peat soil, it says, is really four and seven-tenths meters of water and three-tenths of a meter of plant fiber.[16] The plant fiber in the peat provides volumetric leverage by holding the water in place, like an expanding sponge. In organic soils, water becomes an integral part of the soil. Sediment starvation takes a backseat to hydrological change. "The spoil banks break the flow of water across the surface, but they also break the flow below ground," Gene says. "The weight of the spoil banks compresses the soil and blocks subsurface flow. If we break the spoil banks, we can restore marsh." What he envisions is something similar to crevasse splays, but extending out from spoil banks rather than natural levees, and relying more on hydrological restoration than on sediment flow.

One of his colleagues interrupts our conversation. There is a problem with office space, until a new building is constructed, and she seeks his advice about an interim location. When she leaves, I ask Gene what would happen, in terms of wetland loss and gain, if the Old River Control Structure failed. He says that he does not know. Right now, he says, the Atchafalaya River captures half of the Mississippi River's sediment load. Wetlands are already accreting in the Atchafalaya Delta, forming a new delta lobe. More flow might or might not increase the rate of formation. The Bird's Foot Delta, deprived of the Mississippi River's water and sediments, would begin a slow retreat, with an increase of something like two one-hundredths of a percent area lost per year over what currently occurs,

Gene believes, because of canals. An increased rate of loss of two one-hundredths of a percent per year would be far too small to measure. Overall, though, he does not seem to see this as a serious question. Abandoning the Old River Control Structure is out of the question. But it leads him into a talk about his dead-zone work, linking what he sees in Louisiana's wetlands with what he sees in the Gulf and with what is going on throughout the Mississippi River basin. He has collected sediment cores, taken vertically from bay bottoms and the continental shelf to offer a record of change over time, and looked at the remains of diatoms, a kind of alga with a siliceous skeleton that resists weathering. His diatom data from the dead zone show that there has been steady sediment accumulation in the Gulf for the past century. The Old River Control Structure has not changed this; land clearance in the Mississippi River basin has not changed this; levees have not changed this. This is important because it is a key piece of information challenging sediment starvation as an explanation of wetland loss.

Whether his ideas are right or wrong, they are not, it occurs to me, the thoughts of a two-dimensional thinker. Gene, rubbing the bridge of his nose between thumb and forefinger, tells me again that he does not like scientific debate to center on people. The debate should be about ideas, not people. But for those convinced that wetland loss in Louisiana is from sediment starvation, that losses are the direct result of breaking the deltaic cycle, talking to Gene can set up a series of intellectual tremors and turn solid ground into subsiding marsh. No one likes to have an idea challenged, and Gene's unwillingness to go with the flow, to follow the consensus, leads to swearing. People who have sworn about Gene and his ideas appear unable, as humans, to separate the two.

Gaining Ground in the Atchafalaya

The hard rain of the past three days has stopped, but a fog has settled in, so thick that the stadium at Louisiana State University is invisible from the road, no more than two hundred feet away. Outside of his office, Professor Steve Faulkner and Dr. Matthew Poach move through the fog, ghostly figures loading coolers and boots into the back of a small truck. "This fog could slow us down," Steve says. "We may have to sneak around to the sites from the back side." We are headed for the Atchafalaya Delta, the joining of the Atchafalaya River and the Gulf of Mexico, where Matt conducted his doctoral research under Steve's supervision. Both men are concerned about the fog. It obscures landmarks and channel markers, making for uncertain navigation. Worse, it renders crew boats, bound for offshore oil fields, invisible. The fiberglass Boston Whaler that Steve and Matt use for fieldwork might or might not show up on a crew boat's radar, and crew boats might or might not slow down for a small boat.

"You can hear them through the fog," Steve says. "Huge twin diesels. But you can't see them."

"You can't tell where they are in the fog, and their wake can swamp the Whaler," Matt says. "The bow can dive through a wave, or if the wave hits broadside, a gunnel can dip under water." He throws three life jackets on top of the coolers in the back of the truck.

Steve has a graying beard, a tan cap with a "Red Stick Fly Fishing" patch, and a worn "Friends of Hilltop Arboretum" T-shirt. In field clothes, he could pass for a construction worker, a carpenter, maybe, or a welder, but with a résumé that includes papers such as "Redox Measurements of Soils," "Analytical Methods for Iron and Manganese Determinations in Reservoir Tailwaters: Laboratory Investigations," and "Redox Processes and Diagnostic Wetland Soil Indicators in Bottomland Hardwood Forests."[17] Matt is younger, a journeyman scientist in his early thirties, slim and fit, with a neatly trimmed dark goatee; he is just beginning to build a résumé. One of his first papers, "Soil Phosphorus Characteristics of Created and Natural Wetlands in the Atchafalaya Delta, LA," written with Steve as a coauthor, is less than a year old.[18]

We drive from Baton Rouge to Morgan City. Cypress trees are visible through the fog on either side of the road, along with occasional mobile homes and oil pipeline valves, painted white. For a while, we run alongside Bayou Corne. The land seems flat, but the approach to Morgan City inches us subtly downward. Increasingly, water stands on the landscape; it fills the roadside ditches, and, behind them, just visible through the fog, it stands in pools scattered in pastures and swamp forests. I can almost see the sun now, a fog-shrouded glare through the trees. The sky clears when we turn onto State Highway 70, with the leveed Atchafalaya River to our right and the much smaller but unleveed Belle River to our left. We have driven out of the fog. And then we are at the end of the road, at a boat ramp next to the Intracoastal Waterway, the land now too low and wet to support pavement.

We ride in the Boston Whaler over deep water in the Atchafalaya Delta, south of Morgan City, sharing the dredged channel used by crew boats, shrimpers, oil-field work boats, barges, and the occasional yacht. The sun shines and there is no sign of fog out here on the Delta. The blue sky contrasts sharply with the Atchafalaya River, flowing brown with sediment. A crew boat passes. Steve backs off the Whaler's throttle just as we climb the first wave of the crew boat's wake, and we skip across the crest of the wave, free falling several feet to slam into the Atchafalaya with a fiberglass-jarring shudder, then we climb the wake's second wave, repeating the process. The crew boat's wake is much steeper than wind-generated waves.

The Atchafalaya Delta is not typical of today's Louisiana. Out here, in the Delta, there is net wetland gain. The 30 percent of the Mississippi River that peels away from the main stream at Old River carries its sediment load down the Atchafalaya River and out into the Delta; and as the river spreads over the Delta, it slows down, dumping a big part of its sediment load into the shallows. The flood of 1973, the same flood that threatened the Old River Control Structure, brought enough sediment to convert shallow bay bottom to mudflats, to make subaerial what had been submerged bay bottom. Seeds settled on the mudflats. Plants grew: wild rice, cattail, black willow, elephant ear, sedges. Once the plants had a foothold, they contributed further to the slowing of the Atchafalaya River's flow, and more sediment fell out. Roots held the sediment in place, and the plants added to the sediment—roots pushed the sediments upward from below, and stems and leaves of plants fell onto the surface of the wetland, adding material from above. The land still subsides under its own weight, but for now the balance is positive; material accumulates more quickly than the land sinks. Wetlands—over ten thousand acres of them—appear in what had been a vast stretch of open water thirty years ago, like desert flowers after a drought-breaking rain. It is the same process that built the Bird's Foot Delta, and the Lafourche Delta before that, and the Saint Bernard Delta before that.

Today's Atchafalaya Delta is different than last year's Atchafalaya Delta, and different again from the previous year's Atchafalaya Delta. The landscape changes more quickly than maps can be produced. Side channels, not maintained by dredging, silt in before channel markers can be moved. New wetland islands pop up. Old wetland islands grow outward. What was a sedge marsh last year is a willow thicket now. What was mudflat is sedge marsh. What was deep enough for a skiff can no longer float a canoe. But the new land is not permanent. Formation of one wetland island blocks the sediment supply to another, and the blocked wetland subsides back into shallow bay bottom. Overall, the wetland area increases, but in any one place it may be coming or going, silting in or washing out, building up or sinking down, repeating here in the Atchafalaya Delta what is happening throughout Louisiana, but more quickly, and with the balance tipped toward net gain rather than net loss.

Sitting in the Whaler's bow seat, facing aft, Matt unrolls a laminated aerial photograph. With the Whaler's ninety-horsepower Johnson wide open, the wind is cool, and it is hard to hold the aerial photograph open, and harder still to talk. Names of passes and islands are marked on the map: East Pass, God's Pass, Catfish Pass, Vice Grip Channel, Castille Pass, Poule d'Eau Island, Mile Island, Community Island. Matt says something, but the words blow away, somewhere behind the Whaler. I point at my ears and shrug. He moves closer and talks louder to beat the wind. "Some of the names on the aerial are wrong," he says, almost shouting. "What some people call Willow Island other people call Log Island. Some of these places are named after someone's daughter or girlfriend. I could name an island after myself."

"Matt's Island," I shout back. "But you'd want to make sure that it's a lasting feature. You wouldn't want to outlive your own island."

On either side of the navigation channel, a stone's throw from the Whaler, the bottom slopes up steeply to come within inches of the surface, or to poke above the surface as marsh. Mississippi River sediment, spirited here by the Atchafalaya River, fills the channel, and the only way to keep it open is by dredging. Hydraulic dredges run or contracted by the Corps of Engineers suck mud from the bottom of the channel, like giant submarine vacuum cleaners, then pump the mud, mixed with water and thoroughly liquefied, through a pipeline, to be redeposited out of the channel. Nationwide, the Corps of Engineers moves something like 350 million cubic yards of sediment every year. In Louisiana alone, annual Corps of Engineers dredging volumes are around 90 million cubic yards. Economies of scale make the process surprisingly cheap; for little more than the cost of a can of soda, a cubic yard of sediment can be sucked up from the channel and spit out somewhere else.

That the sediment is a good thing for the Atchafalaya Delta is undisputed. It is the sediment that builds new wetlands. But deep channels are needed for navigation, so dredging becomes a fact of life, an ongoing effort to keep sediment out of channels, akin to vacuuming or cutting the lawn in the sense of the need for repeated effort. Dredging here is a Sisyphian process. New mud falls out of the water column even as old mud is sucked into the dredge, mud from Ohio, Missouri, North Dakota, Illinois—an endless supply of the stuff flows into the Atchafalaya River, hitchhiking in the 30 percent of the Mississippi River's flow that passes through the Old River Control Structure.

Where sediment is moved to has not always been a big concern. Around the nation, dredged sediment has been heaped in mounds along the edges of the Intracoastal Waterway, or placed in leveed impoundments, or pumped away from the channel and dumped in deep water, where it sinks to the bottom. But now, sediment can be a valuable commodity. What was once known as dredged spoil is now known as dredged material. In the late 1960s, first in North Carolina and then in Texas, people began planting wetlands on dredged material. Plant roots held the dredged material together, stabilizing it so that it would not be redeposited in channels, and it made new marshes. The Corps of Engineers funded demonstration projects that created dredged-material wetlands in Georgia, Mississippi, Alabama, Florida, Louisiana—marshes popped up everywhere that the Corps dredged.[19] Dredging engineers and managers, working with biologists, were quick to recognize situations where marsh creation was appropriate and to develop methods that were effective.

In less time than it takes for a marsh to mature, marsh creation with dredged material went from research and development to routine practice. But it was clear that the dredged-material marshes were different from natural marshes. Studies were undertaken to document the extent of these differences.[20] A paradigm developed around the belief that created marshes become progressively more similar to natural marshes over time, but some researchers suggested a time frame of a few years while others suggested decades. The trends that spawned the paradigms were tenuous at best. Each created site follows its own path. Each natural site used for comparisons presents a different finish line. Ecologists could track development of a site and explain why certain things occurred, but they could not reliably predict what would happen next—they were like econo-mists eager to explain why the stock market jumped five hundred points, yet unable to foresee the jump.

Matt points to an island off our port bow. "That one is dredged mate-rial," he says. We have passed a number of wetland islands, some made from dredged material, some from natural accretion of Atchafalaya River sediment. It is impossible to count the islands because one island fades into another, and, in places, what looks like two or three wetland islands is in fact a string of peninsulas from a single island. Matt's doctoral re-search out here in the Delta compared the wetlands created from dredged material to those created by the natural deltaic cycle. He wanted to know if the dredged-material wetland islands developed soils in a manner simi-lar to that of newly formed natural wetland islands.

"This is Willow Island," Steve shouts from behind the steering console. "This was one of our natural sites for Matt's research." Steve slows the Whaler as we move closer to the island. Out of the main channel, in un-dredged waters, he navigates with caution. When the boat slows, the wind dies. On the aerial photograph, Matt points out islands that were created from dredged material. His finger moves from point to point. There seem to be almost as many dredged-material islands as natural islands.

"The early ones are mounds," Matt says, no longer having to shout over the wind. "Dredgers just ran the discharge pipe to one spot and let it rip. The material piled up in the middle and sloped off around the edges. The mounds are obvious round spots on aerial photographs. Later, they learned to move the dredge pipe. They tried to mimic the natural morphology of an accreting delta. They formed the dredged material into long spits running outward from shore, parallel to the current. In accret-ing deltas, sediment is deposited in a front, where the current from the river slows down. As sediment accumulates, it splits the flow of the river, like a wedge driven into the current. The new land is V-shaped, with the flow running along its sides." Matt uses his hands while he talks, pointing at the map, waving toward the edge of the channel, making a cutting motion to show how the current splits the flow of the river. What he describes is exactly what Gene Turner had shown me from the air, in the crevasse splays of the Delta National Wildlife Refuge.

"While they are pumping the dredged material, they can move the dredge pipe to scatter the material, instead of piling it all in the same place," Matt says. "They can make land that looks like the natural islands." He points to one of the long spits in the aerial photograph. It seems narrower than the natural wetland islands, but much closer to the mark than the circular mounds of earlier dredging. "They can come back later and change it if they need to. Over here they found out that one of their dredged-material islands was cutting off sediment flow to the back part of the Delta, so they dug a channel through the site. They did the same thing over here at Big Island, after this photo was taken. They dug the channel through here, I think." He runs his finger across Big Island. "I've heard they called it Breaux's Cut, after Senator Breaux. You can get a boat through there, but it also lets the sediment flush through to the other side."

The Corps of Engineers has entered the business of deltaic sculpting, marrying the needs of navigation and the needs for new wetlands.[21] Like the newly formed natural wetlands of the Atchafalaya Delta, dredged-material wetlands are named in honor of politicians, girlfriends, wives, or the mapmakers themselves.

Steve maneuvers in the shallows next to Willow Island and Matt stows the aerial photograph. Our propeller churns up mud. The boat slows as it brushes against the shoreline, then jerks to a stop and lurches, aground on the limb of a submerged tree. Matt jumps out with a bow line and ties the boat to a black willow. We don hip boots, then walk single file, with Steve leading. Without the wind generated by the boat's motion, and sealed in plastic hip boots, a clammy warmth moves through me and replaces the light chill of the boat ride. We walk between young black willows, with a knee-high understory of mixed plants—spider lilies, Louisiana iris not yet in bloom, sedges, spike rushes. This is a natural island, not dredged material, but even Matt, the youngest of the three of us, is older than the ground we walk on. There was nothing here but shallow bay bottom before the flood of 1973, the flood that almost overwhelmed the Old River Control Structure and changed the map of America.

Matt stops abruptly. Steve, a few paces in front of him, had stepped over a cottonmouth moccasin, and the snake, a two footer, now poses ready to strike, with jaws wide open, gray fangs silhouetted against the white lining of its mouth, and its tail twitching, the nervous shake of a rattleless rattlesnake. Matt moves around the snake, giving it a wide berth by beating a new path through the brush. I follow behind, watching to be sure that the snake remains stationary. We move out of the willows, into a dense stand of cattails. Hempweed vines climb the cattail stalks. Our boots disappear beneath the foliage. Any snakes in here would be invisible. As we move farther into the cattails, the ground grows softer and the cattails grow higher, reaching over our heads, blocking the view. We are spread out now, no longer in single file. In front, Matt moves out of the cattails, onto newly deposited mud, and immediately sinks past his knees. He extricates himself and detours back into the cattails. He uses the edge of his boots to sweep through the cattails, laying them down so that the bent-over stalks support his weight, like snowshoes, preventing him from sinking more than ankle deep in the mud. We change course, dog-legging to the west and then back to the north. Then we are at the edge of the cattails, looking out over a mudflat.

"This mudflat was open water last year," Steve says. "And most of this cattail was mudflat. The island is growing." Steve thinks that a small channel cut through the island by wildlife managers, just big enough to float a pirogue, might be a conduit for sediment flow that can account for the new ground. Standing in the marsh, Steve talks at length about below-ground processes. He is interested in the link between structure and function, between the way the marsh looks and what the marsh does. By and large, most of the functions that interest him occur underground—conversions of nutrients from one state to another, accumulation of plant material in the soil, decomposition of this same plant material. A few inches of elevation means life or death out here in the marsh, and soil processes influence elevation. Wetland loss is a conservation issue, and it is easy to focus on what is visible—the plants, the animals, the amount

of water and sediment. But looking beyond that, water quality becomes important. Wetlands can influence the Gulf of Mexico's dead zone. If the water draining into the Gulf of Mexico contributes to widespread changes in the ecosystems of the continental shelf, as Gene Turner and Nancy Rabalais contend, wetlands may buffer the pollution. Wetlands can strip the agricultural chemicals out of part of the nation's effluent discharge into the ocean, cleaning it up before it is spewed out into the Gulf of Mexico.

Steve Faulkner talks about belowground processes on a five-year-old dredged-material wetland in the Atchafalaya Delta.

Matt has wandered off, slogging through the mud in search of a sampling station abandoned when his dissertation work was completed. At this station, he had laid down a thin layer of feldspar dust. As sediment accumulates on the marsh, the feldspar is buried, leaving behind a marker horizon in the soil, a band of light feldspar against the dark soil of the Delta. He hopes to find an intact marker horizon that he can use to estimate the amount of sediment deposited during the year that has passed since his last visit.

"The plants are picking up nutrients, growing like crazy, then dying," Steve says. "The conventional wisdom holds that the dead plant tissue will be locked up in the soil, and that as the sediments subside the dead plant tissue will disappear deep into the delta. But we measured decomposition out here and what we found was very rapid loss of material—not the slow decomposition that we expected. We looked at decomposition rates with cotton strips and with different plant species. The rates were different for different materials, as you would expect, but all of it disappeared much more quickly than we anticipated. Very little of the plant litter would remain in the ground long enough to sink into the delta." His gaze shifts from me to the water and back to me, then in Matt's direction, then back to the water. But the distraction that moves his gaze is not out on the water, it is under his feet. What he is suggesting could lead to a movement away from the long-standing belief that decomposition in flooded soils is always slow because of the lack of oxygen. The belief is well founded in both measurements and theory. In some wetlands, stems and leaves may be recognizable a century after they have died. In Britain, the Sweet Track, a wooden trackway built of oak and alder more than four millennia ago, then buried in wetland soils, survives to this day. Bacteria are responsible for decomposition, and bacteria function most effectively when oxygen is available. Oxygen is the electron acceptor in a reaction that bacteria use to break down the large molecules of plant tissue, yielding energy. It is, by and large, the same reaction that humans use to break down food. But oxygen moves more slowly through water than through air, and what little oxygen finds its way into flooded soils is quickly consumed as it moves downward. When oxygen is no longer available, within as little as a fraction of an inch from the soil surface, other electron acceptors must be used. Iron can be used, as well as nitrate and sulfur. But reliance on these electron acceptors results in a lower energy yield, a smaller return on the investment of life. In short, without oxygen the decomposition rate slows.

Steve is looking at me again. "Decomposition is quick in these areas with high pH and high nutrient levels, even though they are flooded. It is not what we teach students to expect. We generalize and say that decomposition is slow in wetlands, and that wetlands tie up carbon supplies. And when we see rates like what we found out here, we think something is wrong with our methods. But the fact is that we saw what we saw. And we've seen fast decomposition in other sites too, outside of the Atchafalaya Delta, in bottomland hardwood swamps." His eyes stray away again, back toward the water. "It looks like the decomposition story is more complex than we thought."

What Steve is talking about is a paradigm shift, different in scale and less controversial than Gene Turner's paradigm shift about causes of wetland loss in Louisiana, but a paradigm shift just the same, a gold nugget in the placer mine of science. The implications of a change in the way that decomposition is thought about go beyond an improved understanding of belowground processes. Science is a competitive business—what Gene called a competition for ideas—and although Steve does not discuss it and may not have thought about it, a paradigm shift will advance his career. Breaking down paradigms is the surest way forward for a scientist; it brings recognition, awards, promotions. What might seem like a minor point to outsiders is an important advance within the field. On a grand scale, major paradigm shifts rewrite the laws of nature. On the lesser scale of a minor paradigm shift, one that improves the understanding of something as obscure to most people as decomposition in flooded soils, a number of articles will be published in scientific journals, a few doctoral dissertations will be built around the paradigm shift, and a few lines will be revised in certain textbooks. Nevertheless, it is a step forward in understanding.

Matt has given up on locating the sampling station. He makes his way back toward us, through the cattails, almost invisible among the plant stalks but for the commotion caused by his movement. While we wait for Matt, Steve relates decomposition to restoration. "Understanding belowground processes is critical to understanding elevation changes," he says, "and everything comes back to the pluses and minuses of elevation changes. Sediment coming in from the river is a plus. The weight of the sediment leads to subsidence, which is a minus. Plant material accumulation is a plus. Plant material decomposition is a minus. But none of these processes occurs at a constant rate, none is easy to measure, and none is easy to predict." It occurs to me that what Steve talks about—what he spends a large portion of his time thinking about—is the chemistry of landscapes, a new discipline, emerging from the study of these marshes, that may one day be called "landscape chemistry."

While listening to Steve, my feet have settled into the mud. I have subsided. If I were to stay here, and if Steve is right, I would decompose rapidly. In a few years, there would be nothing left. I would add nothing to the marsh's elevation. So I break loose and move away, behind Steve and Matt, taking the newly bushwhacked path around the one cotton-mouth moccasin that we know for sure is here, then walking through the stand of black willows to the boat. When Steve starts the motor, Matt and I push it clear of the submerged stump on which it is balanced.

In the middle of a channel marked with plastic and bamboo poles, at full speed, we are suddenly aground. The side channels in the Atchafalaya Delta, not maintained for navigation, change more quickly than the im-promptu markers put out by fishermen and hunters can be updated. But the new bottom that lies on top of the old channel is still soft, almost as much water as sediment, and the Whaler can move through it with a mixture of plowing, cutting, and floating. Well to the left of the marked channel, the Whaler finds deeper water, and a few minutes later we land on a sandy beach.

"This is Montz Island, the oldest dredged-material wetland from our research," Matt tells me.

We are standing on a mix of coarse sand and shell hash that was dis-charged from a dredge pipe almost two decades earlier. Although the water in this part of the delta is fresh enough to drink, the shells under our feet were built by marine mollusks. It is not that the dredge pumped them here from some distant location, but that the area is no longer as salty as it was when the shells were alive. The Atchafalaya River flows more strongly than it did one hundred years ago, or even fifty years ago. It flows strongly enough to keep the salt water of the Gulf of Mexico at bay. The ground is firm. Red-winged blackbirds dart through the air, then land in shrubby saltbush that grows some thirty feet away. Where we stand, there are scattered clumps of grasses and sedges on the ground, but this part of the island is mostly unvegetated.

"The shape of this island is not bad," Matt says. "From the air, it looks something like a natural island. But the topography is wrong. The high ground is too high. It blocks the flow of river water across the island." What sets Matt's work apart from earlier work comparing natural and dredged-material marshes is the availability of similarly aged dredged-material and natural wetlands. Other studies had compared recently created dredged-material wetlands to natural wetlands that had been around for an indeterminate but presumably long time. Matt's data show that the young dredged-material wetlands are different from the young natural wetlands, but that as the dredged-material wetlands age they begin to resemble the natural wetlands very quickly, provided that high river levels can flood the islands.

"On these islands made from dredged sand," Matt says, "you can see the difference in the sediment. Dredged sand is the heavy stuff you would find in the river's bed load, tumbling along the bottom. The finer stuff is up in the water column, up above the bed load. It's clays and silts. If you take a sample from the bed load and compare it to the stuff in the water column, it's like night and day. It's the stuff in the water column that makes the natural islands when it settles out. The stuff on the bottom has some phosphorus in it, but not as much as the clays and silts that are up in the water column. And the clays and silts have different forms of phosphorus. In the heavy stuff, more of the phosphorus is bound with calcium."

Matt talks for some time about the nuances of separating different forms of phosphorus from soil. Phosphorus may be bound with iron or calcium, or it may be in solution in the pore water of soil, between the grains of the soil. Two soils may have equivalent total phosphorus levels, but the total phosphorus may be comprised of different forms of phosphorus, some more useful than others from the viewpoint of plants. By subjecting soil samples to a series of extraction steps, each form of phosphorus can be removed, and the quantity of each form of phosphorus can be estimated. Matt is animated when he talks about this. But at the end of it all, the big story was in the total phosphorus—there was little about the distribution of different forms of phosphorus that separated dredged-material sites from natural sites.

"In other studies, people have concluded that dredged-material marshes become similar to natural marshes because of the accumulation of plant matter in the soil," Matt says. "Out here in the Delta, there's no doubt that the dredged-material marshes become similar to natural marshes after ten or twenty years, but it's not because of accumulation of organic matter from plants. It's because they pick up the sediment out of the river. It's a different mechanism altogether."

"The plants contribute to the process," Steve says. "They slow the water flow across the dredged material, which makes the river give up more of its sediment load. And the plants hold the sediments in place. It's a form of succession in which changes within the ecosystem reinforce changes that are occurring because of outside factors. It's autogenic and allogenic succession at once, the one reinforcing the other." In essence, the dredged material becomes the core of a wetland island that is soon coated with the same material that makes the natural wetland islands. This process—the coating of a dredged-material core with the same material that makes natural wetland islands—is fortuitous rather than planned. It would go on with or without the research that we talk about.

It is a short walk through a knee-deep pond to a wooden surveyor's platform. We climb a ladder onto the top of the surveyor's platform. The pale shed skin of a snake, three feet long and crepe paper thin, stretches along the platform's wooden handrail. From here, a large expanse of dredged material is visible. Black willow trees grade into cattail marsh. There is the ponded area that we walked across to reach the platform. There are mudflats. There is a young cypress tree. Despite the high ground, the site looks remarkably natural.

I ask about the value of the research. How will the knowledge about island development affect management? How will the world change, now that a little more is known about the development of these dredged-material wetland islands?

"The main thing is the elevations," Matt says. "It's important to build the islands to a level that's not above the floodwaters. If the site is too high, it won't pick up any new sediment from the river." He points out the high ground along the edge of the island. "It's too high over there, near the edge. That's probably where the dredge pipe was parked. Anything that high won't pick up the river's sediment load. And if you look at it, it looks like it might be blocking flow to other parts of the island."

"That's the value of the information," Steve says. "But all we can do is put the information out there. I think the politicians view scientists as just another lobbying group. They get opinions from fisherman, from hunters, from the oil industry. What we have to say is just another opinion. Even if they're listening to us, they're not going to ignore everyone else. And the people doing the dredging out here have been doing it for a long time. They have lots to think about when they're dredging. They have to move enough material to keep the channel clear. They have to contend with the weather, with ship traffic, with equipment, regulations, crews. And they have to do everything within a set budget. We come out here as researchers and put in what seems like a big effort looking at these sites, then we go to them and tell them what we've found. We say, 'Keep the elevations low, so that sediment from the river can be deposited on top of the dredged material.' Some of them don't listen. They don't see any value in making the dredged-material wetlands similar to the natural wetlands. Others take what we say on board, but even for them it's just one more thing to consider."

We eat lunch with the Whaler nosed up against Gary Island, one of the oldest natural wetland islands in the Atchafalaya Delta, about the same age as Montz Island. Behind the Whaler, a younger island is visible, but only its stems and leaves are above water. It is sinking, not keeping up, and confounding the sinking is erosion caused by wind-driven waves and wakes from boat traffic. In a few months, it may not be here at all. On the other hand, a single good dose of sediment coming down the Atchafalaya River may turn it around, sending it back into a growth curve.

A three-foot-long alligator swims past, patrolling at a calm, steady pace. Frogs are chirping on Gary Island, side by side with fiddler crabs. I can simultaneously hear the frogs chirp and see the crabs waving their claws at the mouths of burrows, freshwater and estuarine animals in mixed company.

With lunch behind us, we walk out onto the island. Someone has set up a target for aerial photography, a blue tarp pinned to the marsh. The location of the tarp would have been surveyed in, and it would be used to orient and correct the distortion in the aerial shots. In more civilized regions, buildings or street corners can be used to correct aerial shots. Using known locations of features that show up in the photograph, a computer stretches and squeezes the aerial image until the scale is the same in all directions. Out here, there are no buildings or street corners. Everything is moving, sinking, shifting. Without targets, there are no known points that can be used to correct aerial photographs. Good aerial photographs are valuable commodities for anyone working in the Atchafalaya Delta, something that Steve and Matt would find useful, but they are not sure to whom the target belongs. It could be a state agency, an oil company, the Corps, or any number of others, all interested in how the Atchafalaya Delta is changing, all interested for different reasons, all taking photographs that are well on their way to being out of date before they are processed.

Biting flies swarm around us. If we stop, even for a few seconds, they move in and bite—hands, arms, back of the neck, face. It is best to keep moving. On this island, Louisiana iris are in bloom. A stand of black willow forms a thicket of shade, and an owl sits just inside the shadows. A garter snake moves across our trail. A stilt lifts off from the water, squawking. A bald eagle crosses the sky above us, gaining altitude as it moves from east to west. A nutria feeding in the marsh sees us, then ambles away, swaying on its short legs like an overloaded mule. Steve says that the nutria have kept the vegetation grazed down here, on this island, more so than on the other islands where we have stopped.

Matt finds one of his sampling stations, marked by a plastic pipe driven into the marsh soil. He uses a spade to turn up a clod of soil, and Steve uses a black-handled sheath knife to shave a slice through the clod. Three inches from the top of the clod, a band of white stands out against the otherwise dark soil, a one-half-inch-thick stripe of feldspar that Matt had poured onto the soil surface, more than a year ago, as a marker horizon.

"This one is still showing up well," Matt says. "Clear as day." The three inches between the feldspar and the top of the marsh is new soil, deposits from Atchafalaya River floodwaters—grains from a farmer's land in Ohio, from a swamp in Missouri, from a glacial moraine in North Dakota. But the soil is not just sediments brought in by the river. It is plant matter, too, roots and leaves in various states of decomposition, carbon pulled from the air by photosynthesis—carbon from the exhaust from New Orleans morning traffic or the exhaled breath of a Nepalese Sherpa portaging freeze-dried food to an Everest base camp, drifted here on a jet stream. The carbon comprises something like 2 percent of the soil's mass and perhaps as much as a third of its dry volume, which does not count the plant matter's ability to hold water—what Gene Turner refers to as its volumetric leverage. The soil is a cosmopolitan mix, getting thicker with time, but as it gets thicker it sinks and compresses under its own weight. The plant matter decomposes and returns to the atmosphere. The island may be gaining elevation, or, if it is sinking more quickly than new soil accumulates, it may be losing elevation. Measuring elevation out here is not simple; some say it is not possible. There are no constant benchmarks to shoot from for miles in any direction. Everything is sinking or growing taller or shifting.

"We've measured soil accumulation rates up to six centimeters a year," Steve says. "But the sites aren't becoming uplands. That means they're sinking as quickly as they're growing."

Six centimeters is over two inches each year, a yard in fifteen years, two stories in a century.

For our last stop, we beach the boat on dredged material placed less than two years before. Near the boat, the plants are patchy—knotweed and goldenrod taking a toehold, a few small willows sprouting, bare dry ground everywhere.

"It looks younger than two years," Matt says. "When the dredged material is too high, nothing grows."

We walk across the dredged sands, leaving footprints. The sand is dry. Where the island slopes down, at an elevation no more than a few inches lower than where we had beached the boat, a jungle erupts, more knotweed and goldenrod, more willows, but also flowering Louisiana iris and groundsel. Frogs chirp. The plants hide the ground, but when I reach down to scoop up a handful of soil, it is damp, noticeably wetter than the soil of the higher ground, but still sand, still too high to be overtopped by sediment-laden floodwaters. Without the sediment from floodwaters, the island will sink. When it sinks low enough to be overtopped by floodwaters, sediment from the river will be deposited on top of the sand. The sinking will slow down and perhaps stop. The sand at the surface will be replaced by silt. The site will become a tick mark of wetland gain in the coastal Louisiana ledger book.

Watching the Marsh Sink

Don Cahoon wears gold wire-rimmed glasses and a white-collared shirt, with two pens in the breast pocket. He is in his forties, with neatly trimmed dark hair combed to one side. Unlike most scientists, he looks like a scientist—a straight arrow, a rational man, a thinker. But frequently, perhaps every ten or fifteen minutes, he shatters his appearance by breaking into a deep belly laugh over the smallest of jokes, with his head thrown back slightly, inviting anyone in earshot to laugh with him. For those who work with him, he is universally well liked. His field crew recently chipped in to buy him a custom-made scaled-down model of a Sediment Elevation Table, a desk-ornament version of the instrument that he uses to measure subtle changes in marsh elevations. The Sediment Elevation Table is nothing more than an aluminum arm extending horizontally from a post, with a square plate or table at the end of the arm, through which measuring pins extend downward to the marsh surface. The scaled-down Sediment Elevation Table sits next to Don's computer. He claims that he can use it to measure changes in the elevation of accumulating paperwork on his desk.

Outside Don's office, in the hallway of the National Wetlands Research Center in Lafayette, Louisiana, we talk about ways to measure small changes in marsh elevation, to get at the question of accretion versus subsidence, marsh gain versus marsh loss. A display poster hanging on the wall, a leftover from a scientific meeting, explains one aspect of Don's work. Don stands with his back to the poster, elaborating, a patient teacher, waiting for me to absorb important points, watching to see if I understand, repeating what I am too slow to catch. But now, several minutes after the last belly laugh, when I ask about surveying the elevations of his research stations, he leans toward me, suddenly agitated. "Traditional surveying just doesn't work," he says. His weight shifts forward, to the foot closest to me. His hands reach out before him, gesturing in explanation, but then tensing.

"Everything in coastal Louisiana is moving," he says. "Everyone knows that. Benchmarks, even when they're available, aren't stable. And in most marshes the ground is too soft to get good readings. But they keep using traditional survey methods. Traditional surveying to track elevations in Louisiana marshes is a waste of money. Worse than that, in the end we don't know what we have. Two or three years into a project, and we don't know if the elevation is increasing or decreasing." With this point clarified, his weight shifts back to both feet, his hands drop to his sides, his eyes relax. He becomes again a patient teacher.

It is easy to understand his passion. In coastal Louisiana, where almost nothing about marsh restoration is clear, one fact stands out: elevation matters. Marshes disappear because their elevation decreases relative to sea level, and restoration requires increased elevations. Subtle elevation differences are important. Inches matter on this pancake-flat coastal landscape. Despite satellite technologies, it remains difficult to measure accurate elevations in remote areas throughout the United States. In coastal Louisiana, where ground surface movement mocks the very concept of permanent benchmarks, it is all but impossible. The traditional surveyor, even armed with satellite technologies, cannot move through the marsh without disturbing the very thing he hopes to measure. In the soft ground of the Louisiana marsh, the footprint of the surveyor's staff overwhelms changes in elevation. But Don has developed a method of measuring elevation change that works, at least in the sense of determining changes in elevation relative to a starting point. And, for no other reason than inertial resistance to new ideas, some projects ignore Don's methods and rely on traditional surveying. Hence, Don occasionally becomes agitated.

"I didn't invent the method," he tells me. "I modified it. I apply it in different places. But I didn't invent it." And apply it he does—in Louisiana, in Florida, in California, in Australia, in England, on a Micronesian island called Kosrae. Although he was trained as a botanist, he now works toward understanding marsh elevation change. On occasion, he presents his findings to geologists. If questions arise that cannot be answered with the Sediment Elevation Table alone, he collaborates with others, sharing expertise. He has become, because of his work with Sediment Elevation Tables, a central figure in the study of belowground processes.

"There are really two issues," Don says. "First, there's accretion. How quickly is material coming in? By itself, that's easy to measure. Marker horizons can be laid down on the surface—you can sprinkle feldspar in a layer across the surface, then let new sediment coming into the system bury the feldspar. A few months later you can measure through the sediment to the feldspar marker and you know how much material came in. Any new sediment on top of the marker horizon is accretion. But there's also subsidence. That's the second issue. Even though new material is coming in, everything is sinking. If there are four inches of new material, of accretion, is the marsh elevation increasing? Not if there are six inches of subsidence. Even if lots of sediment is coming into the marsh, the marsh can still lose elevation. You can't rely on accretion as a measure of elevation change. Somehow you need to measure elevation change directly. If you measure elevation change and accretion at the same time, you know what the marsh surface is doing and you know how much sediment is coming into the system. You know something about why the marsh is doing what it is doing. You learn something about mechanisms."

The poster behind Don shows a picture of what he calls a bullet, which is in fact an actual bullet welded to the end of a copper tube. Another picture shows a jug of liquid nitrogen being carried through a marsh. The bullet is pushed into the ground, penetrating through the marsh sediment, through a marker horizon laid down some time before. Liquid nitrogen is poured into the top of the bullet's copper tube, and the sediment around the bullet's tube freezes. The bullet is removed, with the frozen sediment stuck to it, becoming an earthen Popsicle, or what in the vernacular of Louisiana coastal science is called either a marshsicle or a mudsicle. On the poster, the marker horizon shows up as a clear white band, no wider than a wedding band, contrasting sharply with the brown muck frozen to the bullet's tube. Anything above the white band is new deposition, left on the marsh surface after the marker horizon was laid down. What Matt Poach had done with a spade, Don does with a bullet.

"Suppose you have two inches of deposition but your marsh is breaking up," Don says. "The plants are dying and pools of open water are growing larger. If all you look at is deposition, you might think that marsh elevation is increasing. It looks like the marsh is four inches higher. Everyday life tells you that the ground is solid, so you don't think about the possibility of subsidence. You see four inches of accretion in a disappearing marsh and you dream up ways to explain what you see. Sea level rise is a good explanation. With sea level rise you could lose marsh even though elevation increased. But another explanation is that the marsh sank, that

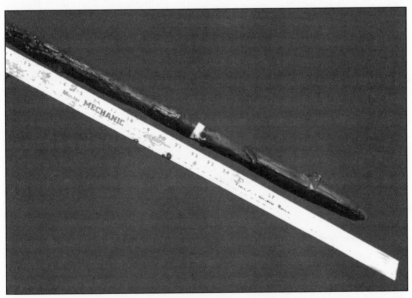

The white band on a marshsicle is from feldspar sprinkled on the marsh surface several years before this photograph was taken.

subsidence outpaced accretion. The marsh subsided more than four inches, so that the new material coming in just couldn't keep up. That's where the Sediment Elevation Table comes in."

What Don describes is more than idle fantasy. Before his work, respectable people thought that accretion alone could measure elevation change. Without Sediment Elevation Tables, otherwise reasonable people believed that a marsh could break up even as it gained elevation.

Back in his office, Don leafs through reprints of his publications, looking for information that might be useful in my quest to understand what is happening to Louisiana's coastal zone. Each publication is in a plastic folder. He gives me copies of three papers: "Marsh Submergence versus Marsh Accretion: Interpreting Accretion Deficit Data in Coastal Louisiana," "The Relationship among Marsh Surface Topography, Hydroperiod, and Soil Accretion in a Deteriorating Louisiana Salt Marsh," and "Estimating Shallow Subsidence in Microtidal Salt Marshes of the Southeastern United States."[22] Then he sits down, puts his feet up on his desk and his hands behind his head, and talks about subsidence and accretion. The office is cramped, no bigger than a large cubicle, but crammed full of books and papers, with barely enough room for him to stretch out in this manner. A green army jacket hangs on the door. Lying on the floor beneath the jacket is a pair of rubber boots, with partly dried mud on the soles. A framed black-and-white portrait of the crew from *The Wizard of Oz* hangs on the wall: Dorothy, the scarecrow, the lion, and the tin man, with the Wizard himself looking down from a window. I listen while Don talks about belowground processes.

Organizing a trip to Don's Sediment Elevation Tables in marshes near the mouth of the Mississippi River has not been easy. We have cancelled twice. On one of these occasions, Don's crew had already driven to Venice, seventy-five miles south of New Orleans and two hundred miles from Don's office in Lafayette, but bad weather kept them from leaving the dock. "Mother Nature always bats last," Don had told me. "Even when she bats first she bats last."

On this trip, too, doubts linger. Mother Nature is taking practice swings. We postpone for a day to watch a front develop, but drive to Venice as the front moves off to the east. Mother Nature, for the moment, has called a time out.

Six of us ride in two boats, three in a johnboat and three in an airboat. In the airboat, an eight-cylinder motor spins an airplane propeller with a black panther logo. Don and I sit on a padded bench in the bow of the airboat. Brad Segura, one of Don's technicians, sits behind and above us, in the pilot's chair, mounted high enough to provide a view over the marsh grass. Both Don and I wear life jackets on top of layers of clothes that protect us from wind and bow spray. We also wear earplugs and ear protectors, double protection that muffles but does not seal out the noise of the airboat's motor. The ear protection isolates us, and the combination of too thick clothes and a too short bench wedges us in place, immobile even as we skip across the surface of the Bird's Foot Delta.

Don occasionally points out features in the marsh. His lips move, but all I hear through earplugs and ear protectors is muffled engine noise and wind. We cross the Mississippi River into Baptiste Collette Bayou, then head south through open water and marsh to Main Pass, and then north toward the Gulf of Mexico. The johnboat is out of sight, taking a different route through deeper water, unable to follow the airboat across oyster bars and spits overgrown by reeds. Forty-five minutes later, very close to the mouth of the Mississippi River, near a toenail of the talon of the Bird's Foot Delta, we pass through a crevasse into North Grants Pond and tie the airboat to a makeshift wooden platform, two-by-fours driven into the marsh to support a single plank. I had seen this crevasse from the air with Gene Turner, a dredged cut through the natural riverbank to a coastal pond, a bay surrounded by marsh. Here on the ground, seven years after the crevasse was cut, twelve-foot-tall stands of common reed grow in patches around the pond. Gulls stand on the bottom and ripples from the boat's wake break across shallow bars. North Grants Pond is becoming North Grants Marsh.

"South of here is Grants Pond," Don says. "This place didn't have a name of its own, so we just called it North Grants Pond. Grants Pond itself has a crevasse too, but it didn't work because the water had no place to go. The water flowed in but couldn't flow out. Sediment filled in the crevasse and stopped the flow. It shut down. To make a crevasse splay, there has to be an outlet for the water so that the water can flow through. North Grants Pond has outlets. It's seven years old and it hasn't shut down yet. The crevasse is still open. Our data show that the whole pond is filling in with sediment."

Right now, water flows under the boat, the color of light chocolate with clouds of sediment from the American heartland.

"When we started," Don says, "we could drive the johnboat all the way to the back of the pond. It was shallow, but there was enough water to get through. Now we need the airboat. A few months ago, the whole place was vegetated. The vegetation has died back for now, but within a month or so it will come up again."

Sixteen wooden platforms, like the one we are tied to, stand scattered around the marsh, covered with bird droppings. A single aluminum pipe stands above the waterline next to each platform. Don tells me that the pipes extend downward twenty feet into the sediment, well below the surface soils where shallow subsidence occurs. These are the pipes that hold the Sediment Elevation Table.

The johnboat arrives and Don's crew transfers gear onto the airboat. There are canisters of liquid nitrogen, tools, planks to extend across platforms, measuring sticks, a plastic tube full of bullets. Brian Perez, an associate of Don's who has just completed his Ph.D. dissertation, takes the Sediment Elevation Table from an aluminum suitcase labeled "delicate unit" and assembles it, attaching the arm to a sleeve that will fit into the aluminum pipes in the marsh. He slides fiberglass measuring pins through holes in the table mounted at the end of the arm. He passes the assembled Sediment Elevation Table up to the airboat, where it is laid on the platform beneath the driver's seat. Around us, gulls laugh at the activity. Most of them stand on the bottom of North Grants Pond in water rendered too shallow for swimming.

The airboat shuttles gear and crew to the first platform. Brad Segura and another technician named Roger Holland carry canisters of liquid nitrogen across the platform, push bullets into the sediment, then open valves that let the nitrogen flow through metal hoses into the bullets. The liquid pouring into the bullets hisses and ice forms on the outside of the metal tubes. Brian carries the Sediment Elevation Table—the delicate unit—across flexing planks on the platform, then lowers it onto the pipe extending up from the marsh. He rotates it so that it falls into a notch cut in the top of the pipe, then levels it using bubble levels built into the top of its arm. At the end of the arm, the table is now parallel to the marsh surface, at the same elevation that it had been when previous measurements were taken. The nine fiberglass pins extend through the table, and Brian lowers them into place on the marsh floor, one at a time. Through the shallow water, I see the two-inch feet at the lower ends of the measuring pins kick up tiny clouds of silt. Brian lays a measuring stick next to the pins to measure their height above the table. "Six hundred and forty millimeters," he calls out, "639, 647, 642." Don, standing next to me in the boat, writes the numbers into a notebook. When the measurements are recorded, Brian slides the pins back up, rotates the Sediment Elevation Table to a new position, and relevels the arm.

"Things seldom work out as nicely as they should," Don tells me. "Erosion can wash away marker horizons, hurricanes wipe out plots, funding can fall through. Then there are statistical issues that come up—how to deal with all the numbers. And I still have people arguing about the stability of the pipe. Especially geologists. They just don't want to believe that the pipes are stable. They have a good point. Is the pipe stable? What I mean by stable is that the pipes are not moving within the zone of shallow subsidence. The pipes should be stable relative to one another. To confirm this, we use a laser level to check the pipes every year or so. They're either not moving at all or they're moving at exactly the same rate. The movement below the pipe, what I call deep subsidence, is not what we're measuring. It's important, but it's a different question. What we measure with the Sediment Elevation Table has to be added to measurements of deep subsidence. The measurements of deep subsidence don't capture shallow subsidence, so the two need to be added."

Roger pulls a bullet from the marsh. It comes up as a marshsicle, a stick

The Sediment Elevation Table set up at North Grants Pond

of frozen mud. Six inches from the top of the marshsicle, a white stripestands out. "These are my best plots," Don says. "The marker horizons I get out here are as nice as any in the world."

Roger measures the distance from the top of the marshsicle to the marker horizon and calls it out to Don. Don fishes a camera from a waterproof box and steps from the boat onto the platform, and Roger holds the marshsicle in front of his pant's leg to provide a dark background. "My thigh is famous," Roger says. "It's in pictures of marker horizons from around the nation."

Brian calls out more numbers from the Sediment Elevation Table, and both Roger and Brad find more marker horizons. After forty-five minutes, while the crew packs up, Don compares measurements with those of an earlier visit. "We've got big changes," he says. "The first pin is down three millimeters. The second is down four. Then down eleven. Up twenty-three. Up twenty-two. Up eighteen."

What he calls big, though, is relative. Twenty-three millimeters is slightly less than one inch. The footprint of an egret could be as much as a quarter-inch deep. The depressions left by geese feeding on marsh vegetation are perhaps six inches deep.

"As the sediment surface gets higher," Don says, "I believe the sediment deposition rate will slow down. It won't be flooded as often so the sediment deposition rate will have to slow down. The plants will come in, but how much difference will that make? That's one of the key questions. People will tell you that vegetation by itself can save the marsh. I don't know if that's true. The plants may be more like a carpet that holds the sediment together without really contributing to elevation. For the elevation to increase, you need sediment deposition—you need water carrying sediment onto the marsh. The marsh should stabilize at an elevation just above the water level. If it subsides below the water level, new sediment deposition will build it back up. But once it gets to the water level, it stops building up. That's what I think we'll see. A key question is how the curve of elevation change alters as a marsh becomes vegetated. Is Louisiana marsh loss an issue of sediment or an issue of vegetation or both? And as the marsh ages, as the system changes, does the roll of vegetation change? What's more important—building land with sediment or building land from new root matter and leaves that grow on the marsh?"

Soon after the opening of the North Grants Pond crevasse, there had been attempts to measure elevation change using traditional survey methods. A theodolite had been mounted on a platform in the marsh and surveyors measured elevations at hundreds of random points around North Grants Pond. Don, of course, had no part in any of this. The surveyors discovered that the pond bottom and marsh were too soft and too irregular for traditional surveying, and they called Don.

"We instrumented the site in October and November of 1994," Don says. These are dates that Don knows off the top of his head. "Since then, we've taken fifteen sets of measurements. Vegetation started coming in two years ago, in patches."

We have just pulled up to a new platform. The water around the platform is too shallow to float the airboat, so the boat sits beached on mud. The combination of subsidence and accretion has buried the original planks of this platform, and Don's crew has replaced them with newer planks. Roger and Brad drag liquid nitrogen canisters onto the platform while Brian sets up the Sediment Elevation Table. They have done this

73

frequently enough to have a system in place, and they are adept at moving around one another on the planks, at stepping over the Sediment Elevation Table's arm and skirting around the canisters of liquid nitrogen. Across the marsh, Jim Lynch, one of Don's crew members, hammers new planks into place on a wooden platform. Farther back, hidden in a stand of reeds, I make out a small unmanned oil platform. From the oil platform, the noise of escaping compressed air crosses the marsh to mix with the noise of Jim's hammering, and, from all around us, of gulls laughing. After a few minutes, all of the other noises are drowned by the loud hiss of flowing liquid nitrogen.

I probe Don about the role of science in saving Louisiana's coastal wetlands. "Gene Turner," I say, "describes science as a competition for ideas."

Don rejects this outright, then slowly reconsiders. "Well, wait a minute," he says. "There are things we compete for. We compete for jobs, for grants, for publication of papers. But there's a spirit of cooperation, too. It's not like business. But the competition shouldn't be about winning, in the sense of having your idea accepted. It should be about coming up with good ideas, then being willing to see those ideas develop or die."

I ask if science has brought order to planning of restoration in Louisiana. "In the early days of CWPPRA," Don says, "it was all about pet projects—pork barrel stuff. If someone had something they wanted done and they talked loudly enough to enough people, or to the right people, they had a good shot at CWPPRA money. People stood up to talk about how restoration works. They said that all the CWPPRA money should go to works on the ground. New research, to them, had no value. All over Louisiana, the bottom was falling out. I mean that literally. There were astounding rates of land loss in the 1980s. The bottom was falling out of Louisiana, and some people saw no value in understanding the processes that were driving marsh loss. Or they thought they knew the answers. Now things have changed. It's not perfect, but it's better. CWPPRA has monitoring. Every project has to be monitored for twenty years. And the Coast 2050 plan is gaining momentum. In the Coast 2050 plan, the state

74

was looked at as a whole. People stopped looking at favorite projects and started looking at statewide needs. So things are better."

From the platform, the crew call out measurements, and Don records them in his notebook. When he finishes, he returns to the role of science. "Science is vital for restoration," he says. "We need the best science we can get to design projects. This means more than just designing the right kind of research. It means making sure the data are interpreted properly, not only by scientists but also by the public. And when I say the public I'm including the agencies involved with restoration and with policy. I've seen people take something that a scientist says and use it out of context. Without understanding the caveats of the data and the way the data were collected, they'll use a fact. They'll say, 'Here, this guy just said we could do this.' But wait a minute—that's not what the data said."

"Do you see scientists misusing data?" I ask. "Maybe using something out of context?"

"Scientists do it too. And that's what I mean when I say that we need proper interpretation as well. The way that you get around the problem of people taking things the wrong way or making the wrong interpretation is by keeping an open arena. You take comments and feedback from other scientists. Too often, scientists develop a vested interest in their data sets. A data point becomes their data point, not just a data point."

I guide the conversation to Gene's ideas about marsh loss and canals. "Gene knows I don't agree with him," Don tells me. "In effect, Gene says that wetland loss will stop if canal digging stops. This denies the presence of wetland loss before oil extraction began. Natural subsidence and sea-level rise occurred concurrently with canal construction. Subsidence and canals are ubiquitous on the Louisiana landscape. You can't tease these things apart."

Above us, a yellow helicopter passes, headed upriver, toward Venice. I ask Don if he is familiar with Feyerabend's ideas about advocacy in science, about the role of scientists who adopt unpopular stands on issues and weather criticism from their peers in order to promote a line of evidence or a new idea. "Weathering criticism is one thing," Don remarks. "But people need to listen to professional criticism. Scientists need backbone to support their interpretations, but they need to accept professional criticism. I get frustrated with scientists who won't accept collegiate criticism. What I'm talking about are people who wear their egos on their sleeves. They associate their ideas with their self-image, so that a criticism of the idea becomes an attack on the person."

I tell him about Steve Faulkner's description of scientists as just one more lobbying group. "I can see why Steve feels like that," Don says. "But that just comes back to education. We need to educate the people being lobbied. They need to understand the difference between a lobby based on a political agenda and a lobby based on science."

"When you go to an agency with your data, do you think they perceive you any differently than, say, an oyster fisherman or a guy from Shell Oil?"

Don pauses before answering. "You can't say yes or no to that question in a collective sense. It depends on the individual. I've had experiences like that. There are people who just don't want to hear what scientists have to say. When I was involved with the structural marsh management study, looking at using water control structures and levees to manage marshes, some of the agency people just didn't want to hear what I had to say. They were using an approach to wetland management that had been around for years, and when our data showed that this method didn't work—that it didn't do some of the things that they thought it did—they were frustrated. They were frustrated by what we were telling them and they were frustrated because we might be telling other people the same thing. And, I'm thinking, well, if you don't like the message, bring up some data of your own that tell a different story. But don't tell me to deny what I've seen." Don looks at his crew for a moment, overseeing their activity. "There are people out there who hate other people—absolutely hate them—even though they've never met. So really, it's the data they hate. It's what the data say."

"When I talk to politicians and agency administrators about scientific issues," I tell Don, "it's clear to me that many of them don't know how science works. I don't mean they don't understand the facts of science.

I mean they don't understand how things passed off as scientific facts develop."

He responds immediately. "It's a continuum," he says. "Some have a pretty good understanding of how science works and others don't have a clue. But to say that all politicians are totally dumb when it comes to science is not a fair statement." He pauses for a moment. "Remember," he adds, "there are even people in the scientific community—in a broad sense, including managers with a background in science, who aren't researchers—who don't understand how science works."

Out on the platform, Roger tries to pull a bullet out of the sediment. He works right on the edge of a stand of common reed, one of the stands that has colonized the new ground in North Grants Pond. The bullet, or, more accurately, the marshsicle that has formed around the bullet, is stuck, frozen to the roots of common reed. Roger, kneeling on the platform and bent over, wrestles with the bullet, trying to pull it from the mud. At Don's request, I move onto the platform and grasp Roger's coveralls at the collar, to keep him from pulling himself into the marsh. It is impossible to know if Don is worried for Roger's sake or for the sake of protecting the marker horizon that Roger, if he falls, will destroy. When Roger pulls against the frozen roots, the plank we stand on flexes. He begins to work the bullet from side to side. The tendons on his neck stand out when he pulls. And this, it occurs to me, is part of how science works. Seeing Roger wrestle with a frozen sediment core that will become a dot on a graph, understanding that the straining labor of a man kneeling on a flexing plank will be translated to a data point, knowing that platforms have been built, that boats have been loaded and unloaded, that Mother Nature has played hardball—all of this is part of understanding how science works. But Don's answers to my questions have focused on the intellectual aspect of how science works, the systematic rigor of testing hypotheses and measuring subtle developments in the field, the open debate of ideas.

The wrestling match—Roger versus the marshsicle—goes for a full five minutes, but when the bullet comes up its marker horizon stands out, a single light stripe against dark soil—data.

"Let me get a picture of that," Don says. He joins us on the plank and photographs the marshsicle, with Roger's thigh in the background.

Back on the boat, Don returns to our discussion. "If I'm giving you a report," he says, "and I don't think you understand how science works, it's incumbent upon me to convey how science works and how you should interpret what I'm handing you. How far can you take this data point? How can you use it to help design good projects? What does it say about what you're doing?"

Brad measures the depth to another marker horizon. "I think this is horizon A-A," he says, referring to the labeling system that identifies different marker horizons laid down at different times during the past several years. "Five hundred and three millimeters. Some of these are getting cruddy, but this one looks pretty good." Then he uses the handle of a wrench to hammer the frozen sediment away from the bullet.

Don flips through his notebook, adding and subtracting accretion and elevation-change data in his head. "This makes sense," he says. "It makes perfect sense."

"This goes a whole lot quicker," Roger says, "when we make the data up." Don looks up from his notebook, repeats Roger's statement, relishing it for its outlandishness, then laughs hard and loud.

After lunch, we ride through the marsh toward Brants Pass. Again, Don and I are wedged together on the bench at the front of the airboat, with Brad sitting above us, at the controls. As before, we wear both earplugs and ear protectors. Common reed grows around us in all directions, but there is also willow and thistle and the golden yellow flowers of squaw weed. My eyes sting from wind finding its way around my sunglasses. At Don's signal, Brad slows the boat and then kills the engine. Birdsong comes from the marsh over the soft slapping of water against the boat's aluminum hull.

"Brants Pass opened during high water in the seventies," Don says. "Depending on who you talk to, it may have been started by a small manmade channel or it may have started on its own. The splay from

Brants Pass is something like three miles long. And it's what inspired the government to dig more crevasses out here."

In 1935, the federal government bought forty-eight thousand acres of Bird's Foot Delta land from the Delta Duck Club, and the land became Delta National Wildlife Refuge, completely inaccessible by road. In less than fifty years, three-quarters of the government's investment had subsided. Had the money been invested in the stock market, the subsidence would have been described as a long-term bear market. Without the Brants Pass opening, Delta National Wildlife Refuge would have become Delta National Wildlife Bay by 2010. But Brants Pass turned the bear market around. Sediment that would have found its way to deep water in the Gulf turned left and wound up out here, in the Brants Pass splay, piled ten feet thick. It was the example of Brants Pass, more than anything else, that encouraged the artificial crevasse program in the Delta National Wildlife Refuge.

Don points to a narrow pass between what looks like two islands. "The land changes quickly," he says. "This pass opened up after we looked at the site. This looked like a good place for a Sediment Elevation Table, but the next thing we know, this little pass opened up. Before that, you could walk right across here, from one end to the other." The land here, in this part of the Bird's Foot Delta, appears and disappears as quickly as the land in the Atchafalaya Delta, a hundred miles to the west. In the balance books, the Bird's Foot Delta as a whole is in the red, and even in this small part of the Bird's Foot Delta, where the Brants Pass splay has pushed everything well into the black, marsh is disappearing and appearing at the same time. Sediment accretes and subsides, islands form and disappear.

"What would happen," I ask Don, "if the Old River Control Structure failed? Or was opened to let more of the Mississippi River flow down the Atchafalaya?"

His answer comes quickly, as though he has considered this thought before. "Statewide, net loss might be zero," he says. "But the Bird's Foot Delta marshes would disappear more quickly. Places like North Grants Pond and Brants Pass would be more remote from the sediment flow." The ten feet of sediment in the Brants Pass splay would sink under its own weight. Less soil from Minnesota, from the Dakotas, from Tennessee would settle out around the feet of Don's Sediment Elevation Tables at North Grants Pond. Delta National Wildlife Refuge would return again to bear market trends, to becoming Delta National Wildlife Bay.

"You can pick any method of restoration and someone will advocate it," Don says. "Someone will advocate it and someone else will fight it. Crevasses build land, but oystermen don't like crevasses. The crevasses let sediment move into bays, and that's no good for oysters. That's an example. Even with good data, with clear data, deciding on the right thing to do may not be easy. And data aren't always clear. The test opening of the Bonnet Carre spillway is an example. The Bonnet Carre spillway is really intended for flood control, but it was opened to let Mississippi River water flow into Lake Pontchartrain. This was seen as a test for the planned Bonnet Carre freshwater diversion restoration project. Some people were worried that nutrient loads in Mississippi River water would cause excessive algae growth in the lake. After the opening, the response by the lake just wasn't clear."

Although I do not raise the point with Don, Gene Turner believed he had seen clear results of the test opening of the Bonnet Carre—Gene had cited the test opening as an example of one of his less popular predictions proving true. The Lake Pontchartrain Basin Foundation, a nonprofit conservation organization, is also concerned about passing Mississippi River water through the lake.

Before I put in my earplugs, preparing for the engine, Don adds one last comment. "The CWPPRA program requires twenty years of monitoring for every site," he says. "People in general are looking for the right answer. There's an honest desire to protect this resource."

We ride again for a few minutes. Brad noses the boat into shore, in a stand of reed reaching fifteen feet tall. The motor stutters and coughs, dieseling when he shuts it down. Before Don and I remove our earplugs and ear protectors, Brad has moved around us and stepped off the bow of the boat into what I think at first must be soft mud, but then I see that he has stepped onto a boardwalk, just one plank wide, hidden in the reeds. Don and I follow. The planks sag and spring under our weight. Within a few steps, the boat and water disappear behind the reeds, and we come to a platform at the end of the boardwalk. At the edge of the platform stands an aluminum pipe, obviously meant to hold a Sediment Elevation Table.

"All of this is less than twenty-two years old," Don says, gesturing broadly at the marsh. "I wish we had twenty-two years of elevation data, but we don't. We've only just begun to collect data." There is little to see, other than the pipe hidden by reeds. We stand for a moment, silently contemplating the pipe. Blackbirds sing in the reeds.

"The crevasse that opened up at Brants Pass has led to more marsh formation than any of the artificial crevasses put in for the purpose of marsh restoration," Don says. "The manmade crevasses are smaller. Now there's talk of opening a big crevasse at Channel Armor Gap, a place named for all of the shoreline protection works put along the side of the channel. The frustrating thing is that they plan to use traditional surveying methods to track the restoration."

I envision surveyors setting up stations within stands of reed, trampling the very sediments that they hope to measure, wandering around lost, unable to see above the vegetation. I think, too, of Don's frustration when he told me, in the hallway next to his office, that traditional surveying in coastal Louisiana does not work.

"Sediment Elevation Tables would be less expensive," he says, "and they would give meaningful data."

I ask Don if he believes CWPPRA can restore Louisiana's wetlands. "I'm optimistic," he says. "I'm not saying right now that CWPPRA is going to restore coastal Louisiana, but it gives us a mechanism. And that's something we didn't have before. People still argue about how we should do things, and that's a healthy argument to have. But now we have a vehicle to move forward. One of the big things for the future is freshwater and sediment diversion. We've got to restore the natural cycle of flooding. And I think CWPPRA projects can do that."

We move back to the boat, single file along the planks, emerging from the reeds into full sunlight. On the boat, we turn back to look at the green shadows in the reeds. "There are people," Don says, "who say that we can assess restoration by flying the coast once or twice a year, that all we need to do is see if it's green. But the marsh we see is on the surface, and belowground processes are where it's at. If we don't investigate, how do we know why it's green? Or why it's not green? Or if we could do a better job of restoration?"

Educational Fishing

It is close to noon and overcast. Six of us ride in two boats. We are
hungry, wet from spray, chilled by the combination of wind and wet
clothes, and, to one degree or another, muddy from handling sampling
equipment. The crew includes two Ph.D.s and a Ph.D. student. The least
educated crew member recently completed a Bachelor of Science degree.
A total of thirty-five years of higher education floats on the marshes of
Calcasieu Lake, fishing in a state whose coastline yields around three hundred million dollars worth of fish each year. And so far, our catch is barely
enough to satiate a hungry preschooler—a few two-inch menhaden, some
grass shrimp, some bay anchovy, some blue crabs the size of quarters. If
we were fishing for food, rather than data, we would starve.

We fish in the marshes and saltwater ponds adjoining Calcasieu Lake,
not far from the Sabine National Wildlife Refuge office, some forty miles
east of the Texas border. We are here to assess the fisheries support capa-
bilities of terracing, a wetland restoration method being tried at several
locations around the state and farther west, in Texas. The Calcasieu Lake
terraces were the first ever built in Louisiana, though they are only nine
years old. From the boat, the terraces look like straight lines of marsh
grasses running across otherwise open water. From the air, with Gene
Turner, the straight lines had resolved into a checkerboard pattern, dozens

of square cells, open at the corners, stretching across the landscape. Water flows through the open corners of the cells. In theory, the cell walls act much like lines of trees planted along the edges of agricultural fields as wind breaks. The walls will calm the water, and the water's suspended sediment will fall out, accumulating on the bottom, inside the cells. One possibility is that the sediment will accumulate until the water inside the cells is shallow enough to support vegetation, and the entire cell will become vegetated marsh. Another possibility is that the water inside the cells will become more clear, allowing aquatic plant beds to grow within the cells. Both marsh and aquatic plants are deemed more desirable than the open water that existed in the ponds before terracing. If the cells neither fill in with sediment nor support aquatic vegetation, the cell walls themselves will support vegetated marsh, and the vegetated marsh, growing along the narrow strips of cell walls, will, it is hoped, be good for fish.

The construction of terraces is even more simple than the rationale behind them. In areas of subsided marsh, where ponds have formed, a dragline scoops mud from the bottom and piles it in the straight lines that are to become cell walls. Crews shove marsh plant plugs into the wet soil of the cell walls, or the walls are left to be colonized by drifting seeds. As marsh restoration projects go, it is cheap—somewhere between $1,000 and $3,000 per acre, if the interior of cells is counted.

Lawrence Rozas drives the lead boat. On this crew, he alone hails from Louisiana. He is slim, with a closely trimmed beard, angular features, and dark hair starting to show gray. In scientific circles, he is known for his work with estuarine fishes and wetlands. He has been employed by universities, as well as the Corps of Engineers and the National Marine Fisheries Service, a branch of the National Oceanographic and Atmospheric Administration. He spends most of his time on research, but he also teaches graduate students. This morning he is focused on the task at hand. He has a clipboard with an aerial photograph of the marsh, and on the photograph he has marked sixty points to be sampled. The only features to work from are marsh and water, so matching the aerial photograph to features visible from the boat requires a certain amount of concentration. A small GPS (Global Positioning System) sits in a plastic box on the boat's console. It is differential GPS, capable of locating a point in the marsh with an error of something like six feet, but entirely incapable of suggesting routes around water too shallow for the boat or through the maze of channels and ponds surrounded by marsh. To navigate, Lawrence looks at the aerial, then at the marsh, turning his head to starboard, then to port, then back at the aerial, eventually drawing a conclusion about where he is, where he wants to be, and how he intends to get there.

The boat Lawrence drives is a green johnboat with a black one-hundred-horsepower Johnson. Scattered through the boat are fuel cans and coolers, along with white plastic buckets. The buckets are labeled "First Aid," "Pump Parts," and "Foul Weather Gear." Just forward of the console, a metal frame, taller than a person, supports a boom, cantilevered so that its end hangs well forward of the johnboat's bow. The frame is bolted to pad-eyes welded to the johnboat, and a line from a hand-operated winch runs through a pulley at the end of the boom to support the fish trap. The trap itself is a cylinder of fiberglass, just less than four feet in diameter, open at top and bottom, with a metal cutting edge around its lower rim. Underway, the trap is drawn up close to the pulley at the end of the boom, swaying.

Seth King and I are on board as helpers, to manhandle the trap. Seth is a technician with the National Marine Fisheries Service. He is young, a recent graduate, with a goatee. He wears a black diving skin with blue arms. I wear jeans and a T-shirt, with wet-suit booties on my feet. Lawrence eases the boat toward a sampling point, backs off on the throttle, slips the boat into neutral, and moves forward of the console to man the winch. He releases a lever on the winch and the trap free-falls into the water. As the trap hits the water, Seth and I leap over the side. Our first job is to stop the boat from ramming the trap, which could damage it or tip it away from the bottom, releasing its catch. We lean against the boat, fighting its momentum, and our feet dig into soft mud. For obvious reasons, it is important not to step between the trap and the boat until the boat's forward momentum has been brought under control. When the boat slows to a stop, we climb on top of the trap. Standing opposite one another, balanced on the trap's rim, we dance a Cajun fish-trapper's two-step to drive the edges of the trap deeper into the mud. Any fish encircled by the trap when it fell have little chance of escape.

Seth measures the water depth in the trap with a meter stick, then collects a water sample. I read dissolved oxygen and temperature from an electronic meter, then take salinity readings with a refractometer, a device that looks like a small telescope but measures salinity based on the refraction of light passing through a drop of water. I call out the measurements and Lawrence writes them down.

The second boat comes in behind us. When we pull away, they tie their boat to the trap. Cherie O'Brien, a Texas Parks and Wildlife Service employee, and Shawn Hillen, a National Marine Fisheries Service technician, jump out of the boat with dip nets. Parcy Abohweyere, a visiting student from Nigeria, remains in the boat, bundled in several layers of clothes and a pink life jacket, cold and perhaps a little nervous in these Louisiana marshes, so far from tropical Africa. Cherie and Shawn sweep the nets through the trap, stirring up a violent froth inside the trap, occasionally scooping up fish. Parcy passes the end of a green suction hose to Shawn, and he inserts it into the trap. Parcy pulls the starter cord on a

Trapping fish in Calcasieu Lake

tiny gas-powered Honda motor that drives the suction pump, and the pump drains the trap. The discharge from the pump runs through a net hung at the boat's stern. Any fish missed by the dip netting are sucked up by the pump and wind up in the net, perhaps somewhat mangled by the ride through the pump's impellers, but caught, nevertheless. The pump turns the trap into a cofferdam; when the pumping is finished, the trap surrounds a tiny dewatered patch in the pond. Cherie and Shawn lean over the edge of the trap, teetering on the trap's edge with their butts pointed skyward and their feet waving in the air while they scratch through mud in the bottom of the trap, searching for stray fish missed by both the dip nets and the suction hose. Any fish unfortunate enough to have been under the trap when it dropped have now committed their lives to science.

In Louisiana, fishing is second only to the oil and gas industry. Annually, something like fifty million pounds of shrimp come ashore, along with ten million pounds of oysters. With finfish, the total catch approaches a billion pounds. Fishing is more than just dollars. Fishing is part of the culture. At least one in three Louisiana residents fish. As an industry, it predates the oil and gas industry. As early as the mid-1800s, the oyster fishery was moving toward organized cultivation, transporting small oysters to areas where conditions promoted growth and produced better tasting animals, in a form of estuarine ranching that developed long before modern notions of aquaculture. In 1880, almost three hundred thousand pounds of blue crab were harvested. In 1885, a man named Yee Foo, one of the many Asian immigrants drawn to the shrimp-drying industry, applied for and received Patent Number 310-811 for what was, in fact, an age-old Chinese shrimp-drying process. Yee Foo was not even a pioneer in the industry—by the time Yee Foo's patent was issued, the pioneers of the Louisiana shrimp-drying industry had already retired. Other inventions for shrimping came from Louisiana: the otter trawl in 1917, which dramatically increased catch-per-effort over traditional haul seining, and the rotating-drum shell huller, patented in 1922, which removed the chitinous exoskeleton from dried shrimp. Later, canning and refrigeration outcompeted drying, and some of the scattered coastal hamlets that grew up with the shrimp-drying industry began themselves to dry up: Basa Basa, Ehnier Dufon, Manila Village.

In some form, fishing will outlive the oil and gas industry. The status of the resource is tracked and, to a degree, managed. People worry about overfishing, pollution, and marsh loss despite the fact—or perhaps because of the fact—that fisheries production has been sustained or increased in recent years. For one database, built between 1967 and 1991, the Louisiana Department of Wildlife and Fisheries continually monitored inshore fisheries statewide. They used fisheries-independent methods, so-called because they do not rely on commercial catches, which vary in response to market forces.[23] State employees pulled a sixteen-foot otter trawl behind a boat for ten minutes, at two knots, covering about one-half acre of estuarine bottom to catch, on average, 391 organisms per tow. Over twenty-five years, 18,012 samples were collected. Brown shrimp have increased in numbers, while white shrimp have declined. Blue crabs crawl upwards. Bay anchovy are up. Atlantic threadfin swim in steady numbers. Spotted seatrout, too wily for effective sampling in otter trawls, spit the hook of the statewide fish census, and their status remains unclear. Gulf menhaden, spot, and Atlantic croaker are up.

But statewide trends and data from individual studies oversimplify the picture.[24] There are differences within regions and among regions, there are differences among sampling methods, there are differences in ways of grouping the data. Around the Lake Pontchartrain basin, fresh and marine finfish are stable, but red drum are increasing in the eastern part of the basin, and oysters may be declining. For Breton Sound, the Barataria basin, and the Bird's Foot Delta, marine species increase as freshwater species decrease in response to marsh loss, increased areas of bay bottom, and increased salinity. For the Terrebonne, Atchafalaya, and Bayou Lafourche basins, there are both increases and decreases that seem to be related to landscape and salinity changes. Overall, though, the trends show good news. If the past can be used to predict the future, it may be a good time to buy a fishing boat. But enter this business venture with caution. Projections based on changing landscapes, rather than past population levels, paint a different picture.[25] Estuarine species will be displaced north-ward as wetlands disappear. Oysters, increasingly susceptible to predators and parasites as salinities increase toward that of half-strength seawater, will decline. Other estuarine species will also decline, not so much as a direct consequence of salinity increase, but rather as a consequence of decreased marsh area and subsequent decreases in food availability. Fresh-water fish will succumb to increased salinities. Even purely marine fish, which might benefit from increased habitat area, may suffer because they are dependent on estuarine fish for food.

Marsh edge, a key topic in Lawrence's scientific life, plays an important role in the contradicting futures that come from fisheries trend data and projections based on landscape change.[26] Light penetrates at the marsh edge, allowing growth of algae anchored to the stems of marsh plants. The marsh plants themselves grow more quickly, taking advantage of more light, but also apparently responding to more frequent and thorough flushing by tidal water, which prevents buildup of toxic byproducts re-leased by soil organisms and keeps salinities in a narrow range. Finely decomposed plant detritus, flushed from the marsh, tends to accumulate at the marsh edge as deep pockets of the rich organic sludge known throughout Louisiana as coffee grounds. Bacteria eat the coffee grounds, tiny worms called nematodes eat the bacteria, bigger worms called poly-chaetes and oligochaetes eat the nematodes, birds and fish eat the poly-chaetes and oligochaetes, and people eat the fish. Invertebrates occur in peak numbers along marsh edges. Fish use the marsh edge when the tide is in, but interior marsh is out of reach, too far to swim to during high tide, too far to escape from when the tide recedes. As marshes subside, the amount of marsh edge increases. The marshes do not recede from the shoreline like a glacial front; instead, they break up, forming ponds and peninsulas of marsh, forming hundreds of marsh islands ranging in size from a few feet to a few hundred feet across. For a time, marsh edge increases. As marsh edge increases, fisheries stocks increase. But eventu-ally, the peninsulas become islands and the islands subside, until nothing remains but open water. Fisheries trend data, from actual counts of fish brought up in nets, may show increasing or stable numbers of fish because of the increase in marsh edge, but projections based on changing landscapes focus on the next stage, when the marsh is entirely gone.

Work by Lawrence and his colleagues has led to design changes in marsh restoration, changes that emphasize the importance of edge habitat. Terracing offers real promise in terms of its ability to increase the amount of marsh edge—the terraces themselves become new marsh edge within a year of construction. Lawrence's drop traps, extensively used by him and his colleagues at the National Marine Fisheries Service laboratory in Galveston, Texas, offer a means of fairly sampling and comparing marsh edge to nearby open water, and data from this study may determine if the terraces live up to their promise.

Now, out here in the marsh, no one discusses marsh edge. The two boats are tied side by side while we eat lunch. Cherie, no longer warmed by the exercise of sampling, occasionally shivers. I spread peanut butter on crackers. Lawrence tells us about his experiences with the draft in the 1970s. His draft number had come up. He had gone to boot camp, then been ordered to Vietnam, but his trip was delayed by further training, to the level of a noncommissioned officer. He received new orders, again to Vietnam, but, inexplicably, he was turned around at the Oakland airport. With the GI Bill, he became a fisheries scientist, sampling marsh edge. There are other stories. Shawn talks about playing lacrosse, about growing up as an electrician's son in New York, about his father's belief that he could make more money as an electrician's apprentice than as a fisheries biologist. Parcy talks about Fela Anikulapo, the Nigerian Afro-beat singer reputed to have dozens of wives. She is wearing, in layers, every spare piece of dry clothing that can be mustered from the two boats, giving her the look of Charlie Brown bundled up for a snow storm.

We split up to resume the hard work of sampling. Cherie and Shawn, working behind Lawrence's boat to net fish from the traps and to pump the traps dry, paste messages of smeared mud on the inside walls of traps, one word at a time, so that each time we pick up a trap we have a new word. Three short messages take most of the afternoon: "Are you cold?" and "Cervesa por favor" and "Where are we eating tonight?"

Calcasieu Lake is well west of the Mississippi River's discharge, in the Chenier Plain, but it is not exempt from Mississippi River influence. Within the Deltaic Plain, which starts somewhere around Lafayette and extends to the east, the Mississippi River has built deltaic lobes. West of the Deltaic Plain, the Mississippi River's mudstream has built the Chenier Plain.[27] The mudstream—the fine sediment that is too light to settle out quickly—flows out of the Mississippi River into the Gulf of Mexico, beyond the deltas. It carries more than 25 percent of the river's total sediment load. When the Mississippi River discharges close in on the continental shelf and into the western portions of the Deltaic Plain, the mudstream drifts west in longshore currents to contribute to land building in the Chenier Plain. When the Mississippi River discharges far out in the Gulf, at the edge of the continental shelf, as it does now, or when it discharges well to the east, as it did three millennia ago when the Saint Bernard Delta came into being, the mudstream sediments cannot reach the Chenier Plain, and land that had been built by earlier deposition subsides and erodes. Erosion by waves winnows out fine material, leaving behind shell hash and sand beaches on the shoreline. Waves and currents sculpt beaches into low ridges. In places, rivers bisect the ridges, creating curved spits. When the mudstream returns, bringing a new period of deposition, beach ridges that formed during periods of mudstream abandonment become landlocked, resulting in high ground inland from the coast—the oak-covered Cheniers that give the region its name. Calcasieu Lake, like Sabine Lake to the west, is a shallow river valley flooded by the post-glacial Holocene sea-level rise. The rivers now build small deltas of their own at the heads of these lakes, and shallow bars block the lower ends of the lakes.

Today, the mudstream emanating from the Bird's Foot Delta, the main flow of the Mississippi River into the Gulf, winds up on the seabed, in deep water, slowly burying oil-field pipelines. But since 1950, a smaller mudstream, originating with the Mississippi River but detouring at the Old River Control Structure to find its way to the Gulf via the Atchafalaya River, has started building land again, along the eastern reaches of the

Chenier Plain. Farther west into the Chenier Plain, beyond the reach of the Atchafalaya River's mudstream, the land continues to disappear.

This is our second day of fish sampling. It is my turn to work in the pump boat, with Cherie and Seth. Shawn and Parcy have joined Lawrence in the trap boat. We move through marsh channels at full throttle, behind Lawrence's boat, with no more than a few feet of water between the marsh edge and the boats. We follow close enough to Lawrence's boat that there is a real possibility of collision, especially if Lawrence's boat goes aground. Cherie mentions this to Seth, who is driving, and although he nods he does not slow down; he may not have heard what Cherie said over the outboard's noise, or her words may have been lost in the wind, or he may not have seen this as a problem. Cherie does not press the issue, in part because Lawrence's boat is faster than ours and the gap between the two boats grows even though we have not slowed.

From my seat just forward of the console, I watch Lawrence guide his boat around curves in the marsh channel. His wake moves through the marsh. The waves themselves disappear under the marsh canopy, but the green tops of marsh grass sway as the wake propagates through the grass.

For a moment, the marsh in front of the boat extends unbroken to the horizon, but then we turn a corner, and a tree line, perhaps a mile away and just visible through the haze, runs across the marsh. The tree line marks the high ground of a road, built on a chenier crest. On the Deltaic Plain, cities start on the high ground of natural levees—New Orleans, Morgan City, Houma, Thibodaux. Likewise, on the Chenier Plain cities take advantage of natural high ground—Cameron and Grand Chenier stand on the high ground of beach ridges that developed during periods of mudstream abandonment. But some cities are built on fast land—land enclosed by human-built levees and drained by pumping and ditching. Roads, too, are often built on fill placed on ground that, in its natural state, would be too wet for traffic. Fast land and roads built on fill can redirect water flows, changing salinities by trapping freshwater or blocking tidal water, impacting areas far beyond the actual footprint of the fill, just as canals and their spoil banks do.

The marsh channel turns again, and I am once more facing an expanse of marsh that stretches to the horizon, forming a line of green against a gray overcast sky. At this speed, the boat skids on the water surface when we round corners. Seth compensates by riding close to the inside edge of curves, leaving as much space as possible for the boat to skid across the channel, but at an unusually narrow spot the skid carries the boat up into the marsh grass. We go from full throttle to full stop in a dozen yards. The deceleration throws me forward off of my seat, and I land on my knees, with my hands on the forward gunnel. A fuel can and a cooler crash into my back. A tricolored heron, disturbed by the ruckus, takes to the air. The boat rests several feet from the channel, beached on smooth cordgrass, but the only injury is to Seth's pride. We push the boat back into the channel and resume at a slower speed, only accelerating to full throttle after we reach an open expanse of water in a marsh pond too deep for vegetation. The pond extends some distance through the marsh, for what must be hundreds of acres, but with irregular edges and occasional islands of marsh grass making its size difficult to estimate.

By the time we catch up with Lawrence, he has dropped the first trap inside of a terrace cell. We enter the cell through one of its corner openings, then approach with the fish trap on our port side, where the suction hose is stored, and downwind from the trap, so that the boat will not be blown into the trap while we work. Of the three of us, Cherie is the experienced one; Seth and I had spent the previous day in Lawrence's boat, setting and picking up traps, while Cherie had spent the day on the pumping boat with Shawn and Parcy. On top of this, Cherie had worked with Lawrence for several years before moving on to her current job, and she had used drop traps in many settings. She explains that it is useful to develop a routine, so as not to forget important steps in the process. We agree that Seth will continue to drive the boat, while Cherie and I will work in the water, removing the fish.

Following Cherie's lead, I lay a boat cushion across the top edge of the trap, then lean against the cushion and reach down into the trap with my net. To reach the bottom of the trap, I support my weight on the cushion. Cherie is on the opposite side of the trap, and on her word we sweep the nets through the water with ten jabbing passes each. The nets bring up a few tiny menhaden and a small crab. Cherie dumps her catch into my net, and I lay my net across the edge of the trap. Seth hands over the green suction hose, which I run behind my back and into the trap. He pulls the starter cord on the suction pump's motor and the motor sputters into life. For a moment, I can simply hold the hose loosely over the side of the trap. It sucks weakly until it is fully primed, then the motor strains and the suction grows stronger. The water level inside the trap drops until I have to lean far over the trap's edge, again suspending my weight on the trap. Outside of the trap, my feet are several inches off the bottom, but still under water. As the water level continues to drop, I squirm farther forward on the trap, until I am almost standing on my head inside of the trap, both hands grasping the hose as it digs its way into the now exposed sediment in the bottom of the trap. I am so far into the trap that my feet point upward. Blood rushes to my head, which is now well below the waterline, deep inside the pumped-out trap. Hydrogen sulfide liberated from the mud gives the air inside the trap the smell of rotten eggs and sewage. The hose digs into the mud, forming a depression that becomes the low spot inside the trap, and the water draining into the hose at the bottom of the depression forms a whirlpool. From above, Cherie advises me to move the hose away from the edge of the trap, so that I do not dig a tunnel that extends under the trap's wall. Her voice echoes inside the trap. The hose, now sucking a mix of water, mud, and air, makes a slurping sound, similar to the sound of a dentist's suctioning tool, only louder. Water seeps into the trap through animal burrows in the bottom, and through the sediment at the edge of the trap, but the suction hose easily keeps pace. Cherie joins me, head down in the trap. She rakes her fingers across the sediment at the bottom of the trap. Unconsolidated ooze sits on top of a firm bottom, with the slick feeling of wet clay. Cherie's fingers leave tracks in the mud.

"It's important to sweep through the bottom, especially around the edges of the trap," she tells me. "You'll be surprised by what you can find hiding in the mud."

Our heads are so close together that I can feel her breath when she speaks. A one-inch crab appears in her finger tracks, flushed by the raking, and I grab it, then twist and reach above me to drop the crab into my net. We spend several minutes raking and re-raking the bottom, making sure that no stragglers remain. Cherie grabs the net from the edge of the trap, and when I pull the suction hose from the mud she shoves the net under the end of the hose, catching the backwash that drains from the hose, leaving no fish behind.

Standing provides relief. The blood drains from my head, leaving me slightly dizzy. I put the hose in the water next to the trap. The idea is to flush out any animals stuck in the pump's impellers. The water discharges into the net hanging off the stern. After a minute, the water discharging from the pump flows clear, indicating that all of the muddy water from the bottom of the trap has been flushed through. Cherie moves to the back of the boat and removes the discharge hose from the net, then uses the hose to clean the net from the outside, rinsing away most of the mud that has accumulated inside the net. While she rinses, the pump catches my trousers, midway down the thigh. The suction is surprisingly strong, and for a moment I worry that my trouser leg will be torn free and sucked into the pump, leaving me half naked in the marsh, but the washing is complete and, on Cherie's signal, Seth turns the pump off, freeing my leg. He pulls the bitter end of the net—the cod end—into the boat, then uses a nut driver to remove a clamp holding the cod end in place. Removed, the cod end looks like a mesh sock stuffed full of debris from the bottom—mud and shell fragments mixed with a few fish and crabs. Seth drops a label into the cod end, closes it off, and then puts it in a cooler. A fresh cod end is attached to the net for the next sample. While Cherie and Seth store the sample, I push against the trap to break its seal away from the bottom. It takes all the strength of my arms and legs to break the seal, a combined bench press and squat. Water bursts into the trap, like water from a failed dam or from the Old River Control Structure's discharge.

Lawrence has set a second trap and maneuvered behind us, ready to pick up the trap we just left. The next trap, the one Lawrence just set, is less than fifty feet away. Rather than climbing back in the boat, Cherie and I walk alongside, pushing the boat, splashing as we move. Shawn, working in Lawrence's boat, smiles and laughs when our two boats draw close together. Well inside the terrace cells, the water is no more than thigh deep, but near the cell openings, in the corners of the cells, the movement of water has scoured away the bottom, leaving depths of five feet. Next to some of the terrace walls, the bottom drops away into borrow pits, where material had been removed to build the terrace walls. Unconsolidated sediment fills the borrow pits and will not support the weight of a person. Unexpectedly, I step over the edge of a borrow pit and plunge downward, until I am swimming, with one arm draped over the boat's gunnel. It is impossible to say where the water stops and the sediment begins.

By the time we finish the third trap, less than an hour into the day, all steps have become routine. Each sample takes less than fifteen minutes—netting, pumping, and raking. The minutes spent head down inside the trap, with the nets and suction hose, become a time for conversation. Cherie tells me about her current job with Texas Parks and Wildlife Service, where she plays a lead role in a planned fifty-acre terracing project, and about her volleyball team. She has to be back in Galveston by week's end for an important game. She comments on the absence of aquatic plants in our samples. She tells me about her work history: she had a job monitoring sea turtle casualties in oil-field operations that used explosives. She once retrieved a sea turtle from beneath an oil platform and shipped it to the Aquarium of the Americas, in New Orleans, for safe keeping while explosives work was conducted. She tells me about working for Lawrence. She looks pleased when I tell her that work by Lawrence and his colleague Tom Minello—work that demonstrates the importance of edge habitat to fish—has significantly influenced wetland restoration projects. She tells me about a student worker who once caught his genitals in the suction hose; the pump had to be shut down to prevent injury. She takes good-natured delight in a story about Lawrence falling from the edge of one of his traps, doing an unplanned back flip before landing, uninjured, in the bottom of the trap. Those watching could not decide if they should rush to his assistance or laugh. She herself chose to laugh. She likes this story so much that she tells it again, when we are right side up, standing next to the trap in thigh-deep water, where she can augment the story with waving arms and panicked facial expressions.

Lawrence's research requires sampling in the terraces and in nearby unterraced ponds—the kind of ponds that eventually could be terraced. In the terraces and the unterraced ponds, marsh edge and open bay bottom are sampled. The plan calls for collection of ten samples from the marsh edge in both the terraced and unterraced areas and an additional twenty samples from open bay bottom in both terraced and unterraced areas, for a total of sixty samples. A day ago, Lawrence had hoped to further subdivide the sampling effort to capture differences between areas with and without aquatic plants, but we have not found anything more than scattered sprigs of widgeon grass, so this part of the plan has been abandoned.

The sampling will be repeated four times over two years. In the laboratory, Lawrence's crew will sort, identify, count, and weigh everything that comes up in the traps. With the numbers in place, Lawrence will run statistical analyses capable of detecting differences between the terraced and unterraced sites, if there are differences to be detected. Some time in the future, he will write a paper, perhaps ten pages long, reporting his findings. Two other scientists, whose identity will never be known by Lawrence, will review the report. They will give a thumbs up or thumbs down for publication. If they give a thumbs up, Lawrence will revise the paper. The paper will enter a publication queue. After another six months, it will appear in a journal distributed to perhaps five thousand scientists and libraries, becoming part of the publication mudstream. The skills Lawrence has to muster to complete a project like this include boat handling, experimental design, statistical analysis, writing, computer graphics generation, mechanics, personnel supervision, fish identification, invertebrate identification, budget management, a tolerance for hard physical labor, and, above all, patience.

While Cherie and I work, we can hear, from across the marsh, the noise of Lawrence's boat motor and the free-wheeling, rapid clicks of the winch when the trap is released, or the slower clicks as a trap is lifted off the bottom. We hang head-down in a trap dropped on marsh edge. Stalks of smooth cordgrass poke up from the mud in the bottom of the trap, and, scattered between the stalks, dark blue-black mussels stand half buried in the mud. I am careful to avoid the sharp mussel shells when I rake through the mud with my fingers, searching for hidden fish and shrimp. I capture a tiny flounder. Cherie suggests that we may find more widgeon grass later in the year. She has seen root mats mixed with the mud in some of the bay-bottom traps, and she knows from experience that the grasses come and go. A shrimp pops out of the mud and I snatch it from where it lands. Cherie chases a crab from her side of the trap to mine and it is sucked into the vacuum of the suction pump. The suction hose has worked its way deep into the mud, dragging me into an almost perfectly vertical position, upside-down. I support most of my weight on the hand that holds the suction hose. Whatever I catch in my free hand, I pass off to Cherie, and she drops it into the net. Passing off small squirming fish and shrimp requires a certain amount of care. Occasionally, the catch flops back into the trap and has to be recaptured. The traps near the marsh edge take more time than those on open bay bottom. They have more shrimp than the traps on bay bottom and the mussels that grow near the marsh edge prevent wild grabs after escaping animals. Smooth cordgrass stems provide hiding places. I am upside-down in the trap for several minutes. Before we finish, I feel my pulse pounding in both temples, and the arm that supports my weight trembles with fatigue.

Standing, Cherie pokes at the contents of the net, identifying what we have caught: mostly grass shrimp, but also several small blue crabs, two fiddler crabs, a single four-inch flounder, and one two-inch sand trout. "We're getting shrimp in the marsh edge traps, and menhaden in the open water," she says.

True to Cherie's words, we find several dozen menhaden in the next trap taken from open water. "They'll grow bigger and move out to the Gulf," Cherie says. "You've heard of pogey boats? They catch the bigger menhaden, for cat food."

At my request, Cherie lists, from memory, the catch from the past two days: menhaden, sand trout, blue crab, fiddler crab, penaid shrimp, grass shrimp, pin fish, croaker, spot, flounder, speckled worm eel, skillet fish, naked goby, lyre goby, bay anchovy, silverside, and mullet. A few drops of rain fall while she talks, but the rain stops quickly. In any case, with the exception of Parcy, all of us are already soaked and covered with mud. I can feel mud caked in my hair and Seth has a brown tear of mud just under his left eye.

Seth removes the sample bag from the cod end of the trap. I ask him how long it will take to process the sample. "Some of the samples can be processed in an hour," he tells me, "but others, with more animals and more debris, can take a whole day." The less experienced of Lawrence's staff members process the samples, while the more experienced do the identifications.

A snowy egret fishes next to the marsh edge, and the screeches of gulls drift across the marsh on the wind. As a group, we are somewhere between enjoying the setting—knowing that we are on the marsh, away from the office and the telephone and the sorting of samples—and the early stages of resenting the monotony of field sampling. Late in the day, the two boats tied side by side, Seth complains of a headache and nausea that he attributes to a combination of dehydration and hanging upside-down in the trap. Lawrence has cut his thumb. I have a bruise, the size of a doorknob, on my forearm. There will be two years of sampling before this research gives up an answer.

Good Business

The Coalition to Restore Coastal Louisiana is on the fifth floor of a building that has seen better days, on Convention and Lafayette in downtown Baton Rouge, surrounded by buildings that are even worse off, with broken windows boarded over, in need of complete renovation or demolition. A young woman tells me that I am in the right place. "The rent is cheap," she says, "so it's home for lots of nonprofits." She directs me to an elevator that may be as old as the building itself, that moves up and down at a pace only slightly faster than that at which Louisiana marshes rise and fall. In the Coalition's office, furniture showing signs of upholstery subsidence sits on worn blue carpet with coffee stains. Someone has tried to brighten the office by bringing in and caring for potted plants, but clearly this is one place where deposition of CWPPRA dollars could do some good. From the reception area, I can hear Mark Davis, the person I have come to see, on the telephone. In an even, friendly tone, certain words and phrases drift from his open door into the reception area: "shareholders," "environmental mission," "reputation," "stretching your resources," and "lawsuit." While Mark talks, I look at the Coalition's bookshelves. Copies of Pennak's *Freshwater Invertebrates* and the *Journal of Coastal Research* are mixed with Tarlock's *Law of Water Rights and Resources* and inventory-accounting software. On top of the bookshelf, a statuette of a mountain goat stands guard, with a tiny placard identifying the goat as a "Conservation Organization of the Year" award.

Mark is tall and slim, wearing wire-rimmed glasses and a necktie displaying yellow fish on a black background with pink splotches that might be waves or seaweed. His hair is neatly cut, with just enough gray to inspire confidence. Overall, his appearance suggests to me that he is young but experienced, liberal but rational, ready to deal but not ready to sell out. In the 1960s, if he were ten years older, he might have been a hippie, but he would have been the kind that organized sit-ins rather than the kind that dropped out. When he tells me that his training and background are in tax law, which he practiced in Chicago, I am surprised, but then less surprised when he explains that he has been out of the profession and working with the Coalition for the past nine years.

As I sit across from his desk, one of the first things I ask about is the interaction of science and policy. "It's a mess," he says. "There are two million people in south Louisiana, and about one-and-a-half million of them are drainage experts. One-and-a-half million are also fisheries experts. People are ready to move forward based on what they think they know, and science becomes an inconvenient credentialling component."

He smiles frequently while he talks, appearing happy to be thinking and talking about human nature and science. "We get into trouble by assuming too much," he says. "Science is a process of challenging our assumptions and beliefs, then adapting them as we learn. It's not a monolith, and scientists don't have a priestly knowledge. That's something we've learned over time. We can listen to scientists, but listening is no substitute to being informed and active." As he talks, his long fingers tap on the desk, tapping with intensity rather than boredom. Occasionally, he slaps the desk with the palm of his hand to emphasize a statement or he gestures toward imaginary bullet points.

Science by itself has weaknesses. Left to its own devices, Mark explains, science would study a problem, but do nothing to solve the problem. He remembers commenting on a major study of Lake Pontchartrain, one which would have gone to great lengths to gather data about the demise of the lake, but which was not tied to what he calls "decision points."

Documenting the demise of Lake Pontchartrain, the whys and wherefores of a crashing ecosystem, would satisfy the needs of science—it would be interesting, it would generate journal articles, it would lead to tenure, and it might shed light on certain processes. But it would not solve the problem.

"One of the things we've tried to do," Mark says, "is put the fisherman with the scientist. Put the local engineer with the scientist. Put the program manager with the scientist." The idea is to bring the scientist's interpretive skills into the arena, to urge the scientist to see beyond the need for a scientific article to a realization that a contribution is possible, to move the scientist from observer to participant. "We want the scientists to become players," he says.

"To move them beyond the role of tourist to the role of citizen," I suggest.

"That's right," he agrees. He tells me that in the early days of CWPPRA there was a distinct bias against involvement of academic scientists. "The academic world has motivations that may not make sense in the practical world," he tells me. "Academics tend to communicate only among themselves and to measure success by their ability to impress their peers. But now I'm starting to see real participation by academic scientists." Several times during our conversation, he describes the Coalition as a "catalyst." Much of what the Coalition does involves getting from A to B, which means convincing people that they are comfortable with a changed situation, convincing them that point B is where they need to be. Involving academic scientists in the decision-making process, changing them from tourists into players, moving them from A to B—all of these are things for which the Coalition deserves credit.

With no urging from me, Mark discusses Gene Turner. He wants to be sure that I have read Gene's article blaming canals for most wetland loss.[28] "The Coalition couldn't come to the conclusion that Gene was wrong on this point. We were glad to see the idea on the table. But even if we're not prepared to say that Gene is wrong, we do disagree at this point that backfilling canals is an inexpensive alternative to other projects. Gene's cost estimates for backfilling come from projects where the canals could be easily filled. Most canals belong to someone, and most are either in use or have a potential use. Owners don't want them filled." He adds that he does not think Gene is afraid to be wrong, in keeping with what Gene himself had told me on more than one occasion. "Scientists," Mark says, "should be iconoclasts. Gene is an iconoclast. When he makes us look at things from a new angle, he's doing his job. But that doesn't make him right."

I ask him if he is familiar with Feyerabend's writings about science advancing through the advocacy of ideas. Although he is not, he seems to have considered the principles that Feyerabend proposed. He leans back in his chair. "Advocacy plays a big role in science," he says. "That's how it's supposed to work. Science is where ideas collide. What we've tried to do is move the collision of ideas from journal pages to the wider world. That's what I mean when I say that scientists are becoming players."

I read from a document entitled *No Time to Lose,* a publication of the Coalition, which states that "science has shown that river diversion projects—like Caenarvon and Davis Pond—do more to slow land loss than any other kind of restoration activity."[29] In theory, the diversions will send freshwater and, to some degree, sediment from the Mississippi River into areas of dramatic wetland loss, reversing or slowing the loss through several mechanisms.

"I believe there is a consensus on this," Mark says. "The best example is the Atchafalaya River. We think of the Old River Control Structure as a floodway, but, for crying out loud, we should think of it as a diversion. Once we accept this, we can't help but see that it works." He gestures with his hand, palm out and pushing toward me, as though pushing these ideas toward me. "The only place in coastal Louisiana with major wetland formation is the Atchafalaya Delta," he says. "Davis Pond is a planned diversion, but it's not open yet. And Caenarvon is open, but it's too young to see what's going on. That doesn't mean we should ignore what we know of delta formation or ignore the Atchafalaya."

"*No Time to Lose* talks about slowing land loss, rather than restoring wetlands," I say. "Was this wording intentional?" He confirms that it was intentional. Discussions of wetland loss and restoration in Louisiana need to consider the amount of wetland that will not be lost as a consequence of restoration projects, as well as the amount of land gained and eventually to be gained.

Mark moves away from science to talk about money and people. "The Coalition to Restore Coastal Louisiana is not the Coalition to Restore Louisiana's Wetlands," he tells me. "Coastal Louisiana is made up of wetlands, but it is also culture and economics. There's nothing subtle about what's happening in Louisiana. It's something anyone can see. As coastal Louisiana disappears, alcoholism increases. Families break down. We project a loss of fifty-five thousand jobs. That's one reason why we can have a true coalition, rather than some group of activists. Our Board of Directors is a cross-section of society. We have bank presidents, shrimpers, even a Methodist preacher." The Coalition has, in a sense, an ongoing sit-in with the participation of the pillars of Louisiana society.

No Time to Lose says that wetlands form a barrier between the open Gulf of Mexico and oil fields built inland. Already, some of the structures that were once inland are now right on the shoreline or beyond the shoreline, in what has changed from marsh to Gulf. In 1992, Hurricane Andrew damaged more than three dozen oil and gas platforms that had been protected by land when they were built. In all, an estimated three thousand wells and production facilities are currently protected by marshes and barrier islands. And it is not just oil-field infrastructure. Within fifty years, 155 miles of what are now protected navigation waterways will be exposed to open water, leading to billions of dollars of losses in shipping and increased requirements for dredging and shoreline protection. Because wind-driven waves cause erosion, channels that cross open water can require seven times more dredging than channels protected by marsh. U.S. Highway 90 between Raceland and New Orleans is under threat, as is Louisiana Highway 1 below Golden Meadow. Lafourche and Terrebonne Parishes lost over one million dollars in assessed value of properties in 1996. It has been estimated that just under 3 miles of wetlands can absorb one foot of storm surge and, further, that loss of a 1-mile strip of wetlands can increase average annual property damage by about two hundred dollars per acre of wetland lost. If present trends continue, New Orleans could become a Gulf coast city by 2050, with waterfront bars twenty minutes from Bourbon Street. To insurance companies, these are more than abstract ideas. A 1997 *Times Picayune* headline said, "Flood Rates Are on the Rise: Louisiana to Pay More for Insurance,"[30] and another said, "Insurers Wary of Homes in Louisiana."[31] In the speculative world of insuring property in Louisiana, one thing is certain: As the marsh sinks, insurance rates rise.

"The problem is real," Marks says. "The insurance industry has no idea of how to assess risk down here anymore. A couple of weeks ago, FEMA announced that it would start looking into ways to become involved with coastal restoration because it's a cheaper alternative than bailing people out after the fact."

"It's good business," I suggest.

"It's just good business," Mark repeats, nodding. "This is more than a nature conservation issue. When a road goes under water, there's no question that you have a problem. When saltwater reaches a freshwater intake in an industrial facility, there's no question that you have a problem."

We talk about the projected fourteen-billion-dollar price tag. Although Mark is not sure where that estimate came from, he has seen it in print, and he does not consider it unreasonable. It is equivalent to NASA's one-year budget. It is 5 percent of the annual defense budget. "It's ten B-2 bombers," Mark says. This is one difference between Mark and most scientists: A million dollars impresses scientists, who are accustomed to working from grants and living on small salaries, while fourteen billion dollars, to Mark, is a number that can be translated to real-life purchases: B-2 bombers and coastal habitat.

"The key thing is not necessarily the money," Mark says. "The key is to make a conscious decision, to just stop for a minute and think about where this thing is going. Coastal Louisiana is no longer a natural system. It is managed. Now we need to think about how we are managing it overall rather than in separate pieces, the way we have in the past. We need to think about fishing and oil and navigation. People are part of it. But we can't move ahead without science. Science is an integral part of the process."

"According to *No Time to Lose*," I say, "if all of the currently proposed projects work, about 22 percent of the land loss projected to occur between now and 2050 will be prevented. This means that 78 percent of the projected land loss will occur."

"And that's optimistic," Mark says. "That's assuming that everything works. What that says is that we are still at a pilot level. We should be aiming for net gains."

Net gains may be impossible, but Mark Davis is used to people telling him that certain things are impossible. He responds by pinning them down on what they mean. "Does science say that it's impossible?" he asks. "Is the engineering impossible? Is it fiscally impossible? Is it impossible from a policy standpoint? Because only the engineering and scientific impossibilities are real impossibilities, and even they can change as new information becomes available." His eyebrows move up and down as he talks, and, as he concludes, he slaps the table with the palm of his hand.

Several weeks later, Mark and I ride through New Orleans traffic with a yellow canoe strapped to the roof of Mark's Oldsmobile station wagon, past One Shell Square and the Texaco building, through stop-and-go traffic onto Highway 90. It rained earlier and the sky remains overcast, but we are headed for Bayou Trepanier, on the southwest corner of Lake Pontchartrain, out past the airport. Mark describes Bayou Trepanier as a microcosm of Louisiana's problems, and although I am not sure what he means by this, I let it go, with the assumption that I will learn more in the canoe. Now, Mark is talking about what he calls "market failure" and "regulatory failure." He gestures as he talks, just as he had done in his office, often with both hands, leaving the car on autopilot for several seconds at a time.

"If you buy a house, there may be some trees in your yard. Those trees provide a free service. They shade your house in the summer, and that keeps your air-conditioning bills low. They provide society with a free service, too, because they clean carbon dioxide out of the air. But you didn't pay for those trees. Or if you did, it was because of their scenic value, not because they shade your house. And if you cut those trees down, you won't have to reimburse society for the lost service. That's market failure. The market system failed to account for an important service. The service is undervalued."

Although we are no longer in stop-and-go traffic, he still has to change lanes and brake to avoid other cars, which he does in smooth motions, seamlessly going from gesturing to driving and back to gesturing, without even a hint of interruption in his discussion of free services.

"Government regulations can correct market failure," he says. "Superfund regulations are a good example. Cleaning up toxic waste sites under Superfund legislation may not make much sense as a management tool on the scale of the individual site, but the law is set up to hold landowners accountable for costs of cleanup. It forces them to pay for what had been free. When I started work as a lawyer, tax laws drove many deals, but when I left, Superfund drove deals. Superfund regulations correct market failure. But wetland regulations aren't doing that. The cost of the regulatory process for wetlands does not correct market failure, and because of that we keep losing wetlands. The free services provided by wetlands are lost. We've got both market failure and regulatory failure."

What Mark is talking about relies on the knowledge that wetlands provide free services—water quality improvement, flood abatement, fisheries support, wildlife habitat. Scientists have quantified these services, and data led to laws that protect wetlands. Interestingly, no one I have talked to about the role of science in saving Louisiana has mentioned the relationship between scientific understanding of ecosystem services and legislation. The closest comment that I have heard came from Gene Turner, who mentioned that an understanding of the relationship between shrimp and marsh had changed attitudes about marsh loss. It may be that further work on wetland services will close the gap between market failure and regulatory failure. I mention these thoughts to Mark.

"If the regulators had a better handle on the kinds of things they're permitting and the true value of the things they're supposed to be protecting," he says, "in one investment cycle they would have pretty much created economic expectations about what you could and could not do. Those new expectations would drive the market. The market would then take over. Look at it this way. If we are going to spend a billion dollars to restore a wetland, maybe the smart money is not to destroy it to begin with."

"This is something we keep coming back to," I say. "Wetland conservation as good business. And if the scientific community can contribute to further knowledge about free services provided by wetlands, policy makers won't be able to ignore the fiscal importance of conservation."

Mark extends these thoughts into the realm of what he calls "nuisance law." "Right now," he says, "if you plan to destroy a wetland and the government threatens to stop you, you can try to force the government to pay you for a taking, just as they would have to pay if they built a highway through your living room. But nuisance law has always provided justification for government interference on private property without invoking claims of a taking. The government won't let you build a dam on your property if the dam will flood your neighbor's house. And that's not a taking, because in that case the government is preventing you from being a nuisance to your neighbor. Nuisance law could protect wetlands. Every time someone drains a wetland, they affect their neighbors. If the government stops them, it should not be perceived as a taking. Science can contribute to that process by showing just how much is lost when a wetland is drained or filled."

We move from Highway 90 onto Interstate 10, through urban sprawl onto one of Louisiana's raised expressways, designed to ride above the floodwaters of extensive swamps. We ride above the swamp, through the crowns of cypress trees. We drive past egrets and a cormorant, staring at us eye-to-eye from the tops of trees. Then, for a few minutes, unable to pass in the traffic, we ride through the blue exhaust fog of a rundown pickup. The exhaust might one day contribute to Louisiana's marshes, converted by plants to organic carbon, then deposited into the soil on the gain side of the loss and gain ledger. But for now it is nothing more than an irritant.

A few days earlier, Mark and I had listened to discussions between representatives of a conservation advocacy group called Restore America's Estuaries and a scientific society called the Estuarine Research Federation.

The two organizations hope to form a partnership. I had listened for insight on the relationship between conservation advocacy and science, but had come away feeling that there was no clear recognition of a way forward for the partnership. Now, I ask Mark for his impression. He sees Restore Americas Estuaries gaining in terms of credibility—gaining, in a phrase he had used before, a "credentialling component." But he also looks to the Estuarine Research Federation to offer guidelines based on the best available scientific knowledge. The scientists, on the other hand, may gain some recognition for applying their data to the real world, for moving beyond the role of tourists to the role of players.

"In offering guidelines," I suggest, "the Estuarine Research Federation is going beyond what would traditionally be considered the realm of science. Do you think the scientists involved with this process are using their credibility as scientists to justify these guidelines?"

"I certainly hope so," Mark says.

Mark tells me that opinion polls have repeatedly shown that the public trusts scientists. Knowing as many scientists as I do, and knowing them as human beings, beyond their professional roles, this surprises me. "Look at the alternatives," Mark says. "Lawyers, bureaucrats, industry flacks, public relations people. There's not a lot of competition. But this kind of trust carries with it a tremendous responsibility. Scientists need to realize that their work has an audience outside of their peers. Any time they choose to work with a group, they need to realize that the group is not working with them because they like the science. They're doing it because it serves their interests. And scientists need to understand that. They need to understand the rules of the game."

We pass two refineries, and the chemical smell of sulfur and other substances best left unknown replaces the still lingering smell of pickup exhaust. We pass under a row of white and gray pipelines. An egret sits calmly on one of the pipelines, watching the traffic below. To the right, not far through the trees, there is a patch of open water with pelicans. In Louisiana downriver from Baton Rouge, the juxtaposition of wetland and industry cannot be missed.

We leave Interstate 10 and ride on a gravel road along the edge of the

Bonnet Carre spillway. The spillway, approved by President Coolidge in 1928, can carry 250,000 cubic feet per second of Mississippi River floodwaters into Lake Pontchartrain. To our left is the spillway levee, and behind it the spillway channel. Bayou Trepanier runs parallel to the spillway, to our right, hidden behind trees. We park on the edge of the gravel road, untie the canoe from Mark's car, and head toward the trees. Within three paddle strokes, we are in a Louisiana swamp, under a canopy of cypress, oak, and ash, floating on brown water in the twilight of thick forest on an overcast day. The bayou is about thirty feet wide. The current is only perceptible in the streaked patterns of duckweed floating in patches next to the bayou's banks. A barred owl sits on a tree limb over the bayou. Turtles sit on logs, and a gar, startled by the canoe, flips its tail across the surface. But to prevent us from forgetting where we are, there is a sign mounted on posts that stick up from the water: "WARNING. CONTAMINATED AREA. AREA OF SOIL CONTAMINATION. THE SOILS IN THE BOTTOM OF THIS WATERBODY CONTAIN HIGH LEVELS OF CHEMICAL POLLUTION. LA. DEPT. OF ENVIRONMENTAL QUALITY." Black streaks of some unknown substance run across the sign, leaving it almost illegible, seeming to contaminate the sign itself.

"Someone saw a bald eagle here a few days ago," Mark says.

We turn into a tributary channel that leads out of the trees to a marsh. Dead trees stand scattered through the marsh, the sign of rising water levels, either from subsidence or from changes to flows brought on by road and levee construction. As we move away from the bayou itself, the channel narrows. "I've never seen the water this high," Mark says. "This is the first time I've been able to bring a canoe this far." Shrubs growing on the banks brush the edge of the canoe on both sides. When the channel widens slightly, we take the opportunity to turn around, then head back to the bayou.

"The state agencies don't want to deal with this site," Mark says. "They see what looks like a healthy ecosystem. There's a forest here, and birds and fish. But the site is contaminated. They could dredge out the channel to remove the contamination, but there is a feeling that the contaminants are stable where they are and that dredging will release the contaminants.

A sign warns of contamination at Bayou Trepanier.

And dredging would damage the ecosystem that we see here. They can't dredge without ripping out some of the trees, and the water flow would change. We would wind up with clean sediments, but a dredged system. So maybe it doesn't make sense for them to dredge. On the other hand, maybe they are wrong about the stability of the contaminants. They haven't measured anything. How do they know the contaminants are stable? How do they know that the lead in here isn't finding its way to Bayou LaBranche and Lake Pontchartrain?"

"The knowledge that the site is contaminated and the feeling of a healthy ecosystem takes some getting used to," I say. And I wonder if this is one of the things that Mark had in mind when he described Bayou Trepanier as a microcosm of Louisiana's problems. Here and elsewhere, what might superficially appear to be healthy ecosystems may be in terrible trouble.

The contaminants came from refineries at a time when contaminated discharges were not regulated. Hydrocarbons, phenol, chromium, lead, and zinc are mixed with the sediment. Mark feels it is important to emphasize that this is not about assigning responsibility—this is not, as he puts it, a "blame game." It is about doing the smart thing, whether the smart thing turns out to be dredging or leaving the sediments in place. It is about the difference between good and bad business practices. "The troubling thing," he says, "is not that they refuse to dredge, but that they refuse to look closely at the situation. They don't want to think about it. And if they don't think about it, they can't come to a rational decision."

Through the trees, a shallow spoil bank is visible. "The bayou was dredged sometime around 1953. There are probably contaminants in the spoil bank." The spoil bank is covered with trees that are ten inches in diameter and bigger. In the cutover forests of the south-central United States, the trees on the levee have the appearance of a mature forest. But the levee is disappearing, just as the spoil banks around pipeline canals disappear. At the bases of some of the trees, the tops of roots are exposed. As the carbon component in the levee soil returns to the atmosphere as carbon dioxide, the concentration of lead in the soil increases. And when enough of the levee disappears for trees to fall, there will be erosion, and the lead will be mobilized into the water column of Bayou Trepanier.

"I wouldn't eat the fish here," Mark says. "Teachers won't bring children here to canoe. But the state says the site is stable. And it may not be harmful to humans. Who knows? It doesn't seem to be harmful to trees or fish or wildlife. Maybe the state is right. But someone needs to check. If you don't check, you can't think about the situation effectively."

In front of us, a family of raccoons—a mother and four young—makes its way along an oak limb that extends out over the water. We pass immediately beneath them, and they sit, huddled together in the foliage above, watching us paddle. "It's hard to believe that we're only two miles from the New Orleans airport," Mark says. "Interstate 10 is only a mile away. And we're not far from some of the biggest refineries on the Mississippi River." This proximity of humans and nature may be another aspect of Mark's vision of Bayou Trepanier as a microcosm for what is happening in Louisiana.

In places, we have to navigate around fallen trees, and at one point we back up to detour around a banana spider's thick web stretched across the water. Mark points out dwarf palmettos with unusually thick trunks. He says that there are other thick-trunked dwarf palmettos near Jean Lafitte State Park but that they are a rarity. He tells me that Bayou Trepanier, despite its sediments, is officially designated as a scenic stream under Louisiana law. Then we pass a side channel with a distinctly chemical odor. There is sulfur, which may be nothing more than the natural sulfur of swamps, but there seems to be something more than sulfur, too, something more sinister. It is hard for me to know if this is a real scent on top of the sulfur or a scent ensuing from the psychology of contamination.

"Where there are cuts away from the main channel, you can smell them," Mark says.

I ask Mark how Bayou Trepanier fits in with the greater scheme of CWPPRA. "It seems to me that this is small potatoes," I say.

"This is small potatoes," Mark admits. "But it's important because it's a microcosm of so much. How do you engage the public? How do you engage things other than an official restoration authority, especially if the restoration authority isn't interested? Because we're never going to succeed here in Louisiana if we do smart work with CWPPRA and dumb work with everything else. We found this place when we were working on issues related to Bonnet Carre. Locals kept telling us that we had to look at Bayou Trepanier. When we finally looked at it, and at the issues around it, we saw that it was important. It reminds us that we can't think of isolated parts of Louisiana. We can't just look at individual projects. Some people think the best solution for Bayou Trepanier is isolation. If we isolate it, we isolate the contamination. But as soon as we do that, we limit our options elsewhere. We need to see Bayou Trepanier and every other project as part of the bigger picture." His conversation is punctuated with paddle strokes, the soft regular slush of a wooden paddle moving through still water. "There are issues of tradeoff here and of relationships between state agencies and the private sector. We've got at least three things to worry about. There is the reality of what we have in front of us. There is the perception of that reality. And there is how we deal with the reality."

"It seems to me that contamination adds a whole new dimension that goes beyond CWPPRA," I say.

"Maybe," he says, "but the fact is that we don't even look for contamination in many parts of Louisiana. If we looked, we might be appalled at the level of contamination that's out there."

By the time we leave Bayou Trepanier, with the canoe strapped to the roof of Mark's station wagon, the clouds have built up again. Outside of the protection of the trees, the wind gusts, kicking up dust from the gravel road. I notice a spot of mud on my hand and wonder if it is contaminated, and I make a mental note to wash my hands as soon as possible, succumbing to the psychology of contamination. We drive farther along the edge of the Bonnet Carre Spillway to Lake Pontchartrain. Standing on the edge of the lake, we watch whitecaps run across the shallow water. A grebe dives and resurfaces and dives again just offshore.

The whitecaps cross a part of the lake that was, twenty years ago, land. Around the corner from where we stand is the Bayou LaBranche Wetlands Restoration project, completed in 1994. An area that had been wetland was lost to subsidence and then refilled using dredged material. When I flew over coastal Louisiana with Gene Turner, I could not help but think that the restoration efforts are small relative to the problem at hand, and the same notion strikes me again. More Band-Aids for cancer.

"We've replumbed coastal Louisiana," Mark says. "It's the old joke—'This is how God would have done it if he'd had eight days.' But really we've replumbed it without thinking beyond immediate needs of the day. Now we need to start thinking about the repercussions of all of our actions. It's time to adopt a broader vision."

Upriver

In 1999, Norman Haigh won a national award for his wetland restoration work in Louisiana, but the work had nothing to do with CWPPRA, and Norman does not write scientific papers about his work. The award was for on-the-ground activity, for putting back bottomland hardwood swamps on agricultural land well north of the coastal zone, in Tensas Parish, cotton and soybean land just northwest of the Old River Control Structure. By telephone, Norman tells me to turn left at the John Deere dealership, then watch for the bamboo pole by the side of the road and the metal shop set back in a cotton field. Although the directions seem obscure, they are, in fact, precise. When I arrive, Norman is outside, standing by a fuel tank, dressed in khaki trousers and a striped button-down shirt, with gray hair over a face lined by sun and the worries of farming.

In Norman's truck, we ride on dirt roads through knee-high cotton, still too young to bloom. In the morning sun, the cotton casts dark shadows against the edge of the road. It stretches across the landscape to meet tree lines that follow contours left by abandoned river channels, plainly visible on maps and aerial photographs as concentric arcs, like sickle blades lying in the fields. The trees grow on ridges of high ground, formed of heavy-grained sediment deposited during long-ago floods, before the river abandoned the channels that are now oxbow lakes and shallow swales. Norman calls the low areas "breaks," a term that I have not heard used in this context before. The breaks, he tells me, were too wet to farm. Otherwise, they would have been cleared long ago.

The ride through cotton gives Norman time to tell me about his past. He is from Kansas, where he taught high school as well as agricultural science at Kansas State University, but later he became a farmer, and he has been in the South since 1965. Now he is a land developer, but not in the standard sense. Rather than developing land into golf courses or housing tracts or industrial estates, he refurbishes agricultural land, converting unprofitable farms to profitable farms through improved land management. As part of this process, he takes marginal cropland out of production, returning to nature land that is not too wet to farm but that is too wet to farm profitably.

Before buying this parcel, he spent six days looking at the land, riding the landscape in an all terrain vehicle. Where the brush was too thick, he walked. He looked at drainage patterns, at crop conditions, at soils. While he talks about buying this land, he frequently refers to his partners, and by this I think he means his financial backers. "My partners have made money in their lives," he says, "and they're conservationists. But still, they need a return on their investment." The return comes in part from leasing the more productive part of the land to cotton growers and in part from government conservation payments through the Conservation Reserve Program and the Wetlands Reserve Program, which pay farmers to take wetlands out of production. Ultimately, though, the return will be from increased land value, from buying low and selling high. In effect, wetland restoration becomes nothing less than good business. But later, Norman tells me that his partners like this piece of land so much that they may decide not to sell.

Over a thirty-year period ending in the 1970s, along the Lower Mississippi Alluvial Valley—an area encompassing land south of Cairo, Illinois, running through parts of Missouri, Arkansas, Tennessee, Mississippi, and Louisiana—five hundred square miles of wetland were lost each year to agriculture, flood control measures, and floodplain development. Some of the losses can be directly attributed to a federal government faux pas in the form of programs that encouraged clearing and cropping of land that would never have been profitable on the free market. By 1982, less than eleven thousand of the original forty thousand square miles of bottomland hardwood forest remained. While wetland losses in coastal Louisiana have consumed an area roughly the size of Rhode Island, losses of bottomland hardwood swamps in the Lower Mississippi Alluvial Valley have consumed an area twenty times as big, roughly the size of Maine. Now, the Conservation Reserve Program and the Wetlands Reserve Program, administered through the Department of Agriculture's Natural Resources Conservation Service, fund preservation and restoration of natural habitat on agricultural land. Throughout the southeastern United States, a big slice of the conservation-funding pie goes to bottomland hardwoods, the forested wetlands along floodplains or in topographical depressions or in what Norman calls breaks.[32] This money is not related to CWPPRA.

"The kind of money that's available from government conservation programs provides an incentive," Norman says, "but not a profit. It helps offset costs, but no one gets rich growing wetlands for the federal government." In Louisiana alone, more than three hundred square miles of farmland have been retired because of these incentives. On average, the government pays about forty-five dollars per acre per year in what is sometimes called "rental cost."

Thinking of Mark Davis's statement, his belief that every project should be seen as part of a bigger picture, I ask Norman to compare what he sees up here, well north of the coastal zone, with what is happening through CWPPRA on the coast. He tells me that he does not know enough about CWPPRA to comment.

"Spending on coastal restoration is supposed to reach fourteen billion dollars over the next thirty years," I say, looking for a reaction.

"That could be a lot of money," he says, "depending on what they plan to do with it." In answering this question, in his failure to be impressed by the dollar figure alone, he reminds me of Mark Davis. A honeybee buzzes over the truck's dashboard, bouncing off the windshield in an effort to escape. Norman opens his window and sweeps the bee out of the truck with a gentle wave of his hand. "Don't want to aggravate that little old honey bee," he says.

As we approach a break, the cotton stops in an abrupt line. Belly-tall Johnson grass, a kind of wild sorghum with a single pale stripe running the length of each leaf, grows in the two-hundred-foot gap between the cotton and the trees of the break. Norman parks the truck and we walk through the Johnson grass. Saplings of cypress and green ash hide in the Johnson grass—bare-root plantings less than a year old and no more than two feet tall, spaced on twelve-foot centers in straight rows running beneath the tops of the Johnson grass. Cottonwood, sweetgum, persimmon, and willow have come in on their own, scattered among the cypress and green ash. "The idea is to plant trees that don't seed into these old fields on their own," Norman says, "those whose seeds don't carry far on the wind: oaks, cypress, green ash. All the planting does is give the forest a little head start."

In places, willow and persimmon have broken through the Johnson grass, poking scraggly branches into full sunlight. Sweetgum and cottonwood almost reach the top of the Johnson grass and may break through by the end of the year. The planted saplings—the oaks, cypress, and green ash—are slow growers and have much further to go. I have to push the Johnson grass aside to find the saplings. It may be five years before they break through the Johnson grass canopy. "It will be fifteen years before this looks like a young forest," Norman says. In a decade, the trees will begin to shade out the Johnson grass, and in another five decades, or six, long after Norman and I are gone, this field will be a mature forest.

"Last year was dry," Norman says, "too dry. We had to replant some of this." He scrapes the ground's surface with the heel of his boot. "The soils are mostly Tensas," he tells me, "with some Sharkey clays in the lower areas. But most of the Sharkeys are buried by Tensas that eroded off the high ground." Out here, in this part of Louisiana and throughout the Lower Mississippi Alluvial Valley, farming has exaggerated the flatness of the land. What had been a fairly flat floodplain landscape has been further flattened by plowing, which breaks up the soil, freeing it to flow downhill, making the high ground lower and the low ground higher. Where irrigation waters crops, machinery guided by survey lasers flattens the land even more, eliminating the low spots entirely, which allows irrigation water to flow evenly across cropped fields. Banks, I have been told, are reluctant to loan money for irrigation until the land has been laser leveled. The reforested land supports trees, but it is flatter than the natural landscape, and it has unnatural soils, Tensas on top of Sharkey clays. Norman tells me that the cypress is planted on the lower ground and the green ash is planted on the higher ground, but the difference between high and low is subtle on this flat landscape.

Back in the truck, Norman drives past the planted trees and Johnson grass, through the break, and across more cotton to another break. This break is wider and there is standing water. Scattered cypress trees, eighteen inches thick, stand in the water. Mats of algae and aquatic weeds float against the shoreline. A two-foot alligator eyes us from the water's edge. Some distance away a pipe stands up out of the water, part of the plumbing Norman uses to control lake levels. Norman tells me that the pipe is supposed to be beaver proof, but his tone suggests that he does not believe it. The recovery of beaver populations throughout the South is a credible victory for the conservation movement, but beavers block water flows without consulting land managers. For those who want to control water levels, even in the interests of wetlands, beavers present one more challenge.

I ask Norman if he can still use the land for hunting even though some of the restoration work was paid for by the Wetlands Reserve Program.

"The program allows for some commercial harvest," he answers. "We can take crawfish out of the lake and hunting is okay. But I guess I haven't hunted ducks in twenty-five years. I see no harm in it, but I just haven't had the time."

Norman points out the location of underground pipes and a pump. "That pump," he says, "has a capacity of three thousand gallons per minute. Aside from the pump, the only natural drainage into the lake is from that ridge." In flat Louisiana, topographical hyperbole makes any perceptible swelling of the land, no matter how slight, a ridge. "There isn't enough water coming off that ridge to keep the lake full all year," he adds.

"At times, we have to pump water in. We hold the depth around six feet. Pumping the water increases dissolved oxygen in the lake, but it can get you in trouble, too, if it causes turnover. If the lake turns over, water from the bottom comes to the surface. There's no oxygen in the bottom water and it kills the fish."

He stops for a minute, looking out at the water and thinking. "We've had to treat algae blooms in here, too," he says. "We mounted a seeder on the front of a boat and sprayed copper sulfate from the seeder. It takes care of the algae, but you have to be careful not to get it in your eyes."

Part of Norman's restoration of lakes on the property required rerouting of what he refers to as "the Parish drain," which required coordination with Parish authorities as well as neighboring landowners. Both the Conservation Reserve Program and the Wetlands Reserve Program require coordination with federal government authorities. Norman has also had occasion to request Section 404 permits from the Corps of Engineers, allowing construction of access roads or levees to control water flow. Norman does all of these things himself, just one more aspect of farm management. I ask him if it is difficult to acquire Corps permits. "They know what I'm trying to do here," he says. "I've had them down and shown them around. I think I've developed a personal relationship. That makes it easier."

The deafening whine of a yellow crop duster, coming in low, interrupts our conversation. "World War II engine," Norman says, after the plane has passed.

We make a final stop in a stand of preserved forest. Although there is no obvious trail to follow, Norman quickly locates an unusually large muscadine grapevine hanging from a cypress. In the cool shadows of the forest, he stands between the vine and a cypress knee—an upturned root that reaches his belt line. The grapevine is almost as big around as his thigh. The vine's size reflects its age, as well as the fact that the tree it hangs from survived an era of cutting and clearing. Why the tree was not cut remains a mystery. "Deer really like muscadine grapes," Norman says. "All the wildlife likes muscadine grapes. Even I like muscadine grapes."

I ask him about the role of science in restoring this land. He thinks about this for a moment before replying, then politely says that he some-times uses information from extension documents—guidelines for plant-ing different tree species or for construction of water control structures, written and distributed by the federal government to transfer scientific information to the public. He does not speak of the link between science and government conservation programs, between science and soil classi-fication methods that allow him to casually identify Tensas and Sharkey clays, between science and an understanding of lake turnover and fish kills, between science and use of copper sulfate to control algae blooms. Clearly, he is not on the edge of his seat waiting for the next paradigm shift.

Several months later, after the cotton harvest, I meet Sammy King, a scientist interested in bottomland hardwood swamp restoration. We are twenty miles north of Norman Haigh's land and still in the same country of bottomland swamps turned to agriculture. Sammy, in his mid-thirties, works for the National Wetlands Research Center in Lafayette, the same government laboratory that employs Don Cahoon. He wears laced-up boots and camouflage pants with a light blue T-shirt bearing the Society of Wetland Scientists logo. In Sammy's truck, we travel through farmland, past the stubble of harvested bean fields and the bare earth of harvested cotton, along roads whose shoulders are speckled with white cotton balls blown from fields or fallen from bales. A hardcover copy of *The Amphibi-ans and Reptiles of Louisiana,* with color plates of salamanders, lizards, and snakes, sits on the console between the driver and passenger seats.

"Almost nothing has been done with amphibians in the Lower Missis-sippi Alluvial Valley," Sammy says.

Sammy is starting a new project. Today, he is looking for research sites on the sixty-five-thousand-acre Tensas National Wildlife Refuge. The Ten-sas Refuge is what passes for wilderness in modern south-central America. It is surrounded by agriculture. Even within the refuge, farm fields are mixed with forest. Some of the farm fields are leased for bean and corn farming to help fund operations, but other fields are being put back into forest. Before becoming a National Wildlife Refuge in 1980, most of the land was managed for timber. The forest has been cut over for timber at least once, and in most places several times, each time growing back to a respectable size. A big piece of the refuge was once owned by Singer—the company used wood from the land to make sewing machines and spools. There are oil wells within the refuge. Over the past two hundred years, flood regimes have changed because of both local levees and changes downstream, in the Mississippi River itself. In short, the land protected by the refuge is managed wilderness, where forest thinning is practiced and water levels are controlled. But somewhere out here, in this mix of field and managed forest, one of the last ivory-billed woodpeckers was seen sixty years ago. Despite management, the land remains wild enough that more recent rumors of ivory-billed woodpecker sightings cannot be entirely dismissed. Currently, more than two hundred black bears wander the refuge, and there are deer, raccoons, alligators, snakes, possums, and armadillos.

Driving into the refuge, we follow the Tensas River, a river that flows through a channel cut by the Mississippi River before this reach of the Mississippi River shifted to the east, leaving the Tensas River to drain a local watershed and to join the Black and the Red and finally the Atchafalaya and the modern Mississippi, in what might be called a confluence of past, present, and future flows. Here the Tensas River is little more than a stream, deeply entrenched in what looks like an earthen gutter from the road. In a month or two, the winter rains will settle in and the river will rise, carrying, for a while, a substantial amount of water. But the river seldom overbanks to flood the forest. The last time was 1991. Flooded bottomland hardwood swamps in the Tensas National Wildlife Refuge do not flood from river levels high enough to spill over the river's banks as they have in the past. Instead, they flood with trapped rainfall or with river water that flows through natural channels connecting the river with lakes and low-lying forest.

Sammy tells me that one of his interests in amphibians is related to restoration. On refuge lands, just as on farmlands managed under government conservation programs, restoration of bottomland hardwood forests is more or less synonymous with tree planting. Amphibians may count on intermittently flooded swales for habitat—on low areas too dry for fish but wet enough for salamanders. Over time, in this agricultural setting, swales have been purposely filled and drained, or filled by eroded soil loosened by plows. Tree planting may not be enough. Before planting, it may be important to restore what Sammy calls "topographical relief"— the ridges and swales affected by plowing.

"I don't want to overstate this point," he says. "These restoration programs have enemies, and I don't want anything I say to be used as ammunition against planting trees. Reforested tracts are definitely an improvement over agricultural lands, but my point is that it might be important to do more—at least sometimes."

In the refuge headquarters building, we lay a four-foot-long map of the refuge across a conference room table, then talk to refuge biologists about potential sites. The map looks in some ways like a jigsaw puzzle, with irregular boundaries where the land was undesirable or too expensive to buy as part of the refuge system. The puzzle is missing pieces. It has blank areas completely enclosed by the refuge, where private landowners held onto family land for sentimental reasons or for hunting. Sickle-shaped ridge-and-swale topography runs across parts of the refuge map like tiger stripes, making the high and low ground of abandoned river channels and banks. Some of the swales are labeled: Rainey Lake, Bear Wallow, Lake Nick, Little Bear Lake, Renford Lake. Sammy explains how plowing can fill swales, how soil from high ground can bury the soil of low ground, leaving behind a flattened landscape.

"We want to look at different kinds of swales," Sammy tells the refuge biologists. "It would be good if we can find some that are permanently flooded and some that are seasonally flooded, by rain and by the Tensas River. We want variety."

The refuge biologists suggest a number of sites, then say that some of them will be hard to reach once the rain starts. "A lot of these places," one of the men says, "are close together, but to get from one to the other you may have to drive around in a big loop, maybe twenty miles. And when the ground is wet it will be tough going to get inside."

On the map, we find swales in forested land, but we find swales in some of the agricultural fields, too. And there are swales in places that may soon be planted with trees as part of a reforestation program or that have been planted within the past few years.

Outside again, standing next to the truck, I tell Sammy that I have talked about the issue of land contours to at least twenty people in the past six months—people involved with land restoration—and that all of them were resistant. Some believed that lost contours were only an issue on land that had been laser leveled, which was too valuable, as a rule, to be put back into trees. Others believed that recontouring would be too expensive, that the tradeoff of reducing the number of acres planted to pay for excavating filled-in swales did not make sense. Government conservation programs focus on planting trees and do not provide sufficient funding to restore topographical relief, a process that could increase costs by a factor of six or more.

"No one really knows what swales are worth," Sammy says. "No one has data."

"But you will meet some resistance," I tell him. "These people doing the planting aren't necessarily going to want to see data. They may be satisfied with what they're doing."

"They're not the ones we have to convince," Sammy says, leaning against his truck. "Policy makers are the real audience for this kind of work. If the data show that swales are important, and if the data reach the ears of policy makers, we've had an impact."

In a sense, what Sammy envisions contrasts with CWPPRA—CWPPRA projects focus on hydrology and sediments but seldom undertake extensive planting, while here in the bottomland swamps the focus is on planting, with scant attention to hydrology and sediments. What Sammy talks about might be another paradigm shift, a change from the paradigm of simple planting as restoration of bottomlands to a more holistic approach that considers topography and hydrology as a starting point.

On the door of Sammy's truck is a sign with his agency's logo and the words "Science for a Changing World."

We park on a dirt road between a forest of mostly sugarberry and elm, probably fifty years old or older, and a tract of smaller trees that were planted in 1993. The trees in the planted tract stand no more than six feet tall. Blackberry grows between the small trees and the thorns make walking through the planted tract almost impossible.

According to a questionnaire survey that Sammy organized, most tree planting for restoration uses bare root seedlings, but the site we are looking at is one of a handful planted by direct seeding of acorns. Refuge staff have tried planting with broadcast seeders that throw seeds in all directions, at random, as well as mechanized seeders that plant seeds at discrete distances, in rows. For the refuge, direct seeding is cheaper than planting seedlings, although plans are in place to plant seedlings in a program to be paid for by a power company affiliate seeking to counterbalance air pollution with new trees.

"Most of what we know about tree planting in bottomlands is from trial and error," Sammy says. "There's almost no experimental design and very little follow-up monitoring or record keeping. It's difficult to know what works best. What makes it even harder is that you can look at a site a couple of years after planting and write it off as a complete failure. All the trees are gone, eaten by deer or rodents. But later the trees bounce back, from their roots, and the site looks great."

From the road, the ground looks lower on the left side of the planted tract, where a broad swale has survived years of farming. "When it rains," Sammy says, "the swale will be more obvious. That end of the field will fill with water."

It is interesting to me that he calls this a field and that, without thinking, I accept this descriptor—this tract has been planted with trees, but it will be some time before it becomes a forest, and until then it remains a field. It is interesting, too, to see that the planted tract is not completely level. Because a swale can survive years of plowing, the question for Sammy becomes one of how much the swale has filled in and whether or not excavation would be worthwhile, or if amphibians would be just as happy in what is left of the swale.

We turn our backs on the planted tract and cross the road, moving into

The Sediment Elevation Table set up at North Grants Pond

the forest, walking beneath the sugarberry and elm. None of the black-berry that made movement across the planted tract grows here. Instead, scattered sabal palms grow waste high, and under the shadows of the sugarberry and elm the land seems park-like.

"Under natural conditions," Sammy tells me, "elm comes in after oak, and then sugarberry comes in. This would be a late successional forest, already past the oak stage. But out here, after a hundred years of repeated harvesting, it's hard to say what's going on."

Sammy's original interests as an ecologist were linked to plant succession—to the development of forests over time. And, perhaps as an off-shoot of this, he has written about the history of bottomland swamps, from before European settlement to the present, in a book chapter entitled "Bottomland Hardwood Forests: Past, Present, and Future."[33] Over the twenty thousand years that these forests have existed, they have changed almost continuously in response to climate change and, later, human ma-nipulation. Hunting and gathering by the first humans, who came to the land some twelve thousand years ago, had little impact, but by the Wood-land Cultural Period, from about three thousand to twelve hundred years ago, humans burned the forest to open land for farming. By the Mississippian Cultural Period, to about five hundred years ago, they built fortified villages that might cover forty acres, with extensive cornfields surrounding the villages on what otherwise would have been bottomland forest. At European contact, there may have been as many as eighteen million people living off the land. De Soto described fields that were sixty miles long. This history of human presence and ongoing change makes it difficult to pin down exactly what is meant by "natural conditions," and, subsequently, what we are after when we restore the land.

I ask Sammy if science can help formulate objectives for land restoration. "Most of the planting focuses on oak," he says. "Some of these sites are so isolated that the heavy mast species won't come back on their own. Acorns don't move around in the wind, so only the light-seeded species come in. And wildlife schools all over the country talk about oak and the importance of acorns as food for wildlife. Those ideas came from science originally, and they focused reforestation on oaks. For a long time, all that was planted was oaks. But people are planting other things now, partly because it's hard to get oak stock for planting. And science is contributing to that change, too. Scientists are saying, 'Look, there's more out there than just oak.' It's a slow change, but people are beginning to listen. And the research I'm starting now, looking at swales, at how important they are to amphibians, might contribute to changed objectives."

"So what are we after?" I ask. "Are we looking for a pre-European landscape or something that might have been here in 1850? Or something else altogether?"

"I think we're playing it by ear. We can get the tree cover back, and that's important, and at the same time we can reduce erosion and protect soils. Right now, restoration is just getting something done quickly. We can fine-tune what we've done later. That's one of the things that science can do—fine-tuning. But we have to be careful to credit the benefits of what has already been done. In my opinion, there are some weaknesses in some of the restoration programs, but overall, they're incredibly significant." The idea that what has already been done is significant, and that objective criticism of current practices should not overlook what has been accomplished, is something that Sammy returns to frequently. Similarly, he talks repeatedly about working with landowners, about recognizing that so much of what has to be done will be done on private land.

As we move through the forest, within fifty feet of the road, Sammy sees something change in the vegetation. "Water probably comes up to about here every year," he says. Whatever he sees is invisible to me, but as we move further into the trees, the change becomes obvious, and, abruptly, the forest ends. We stand for a moment at the edge of a thicket of buttonbush, a shrub that grows in standing water, but the ground under the buttonbush today is dry and cracked. Within the buttonbush, in a small clearing, a cypress tree with a fifteen-inch trunk stands with a water stain close to eye level, showing that the buttonbush and even the forest floor, back somewhere close to the place that Sammy had pointed out, have been under water not too long ago. We have walked across the edge of what the map called Lake Nick, crossing an indefinite boundary between lake and shore.

"Let's see if the lake is holding any water at all," Sammy says. I follow him through the buttonbush, on a zigzag path, bent over to push my way through the branches like a human bulldozer, and with my hand in front of my face to protect my eyes. In places, we come across rotting cypress knees, all that remains of trees cut seventy years before. When we come across a live cypress, with a twenty-five inch trunk, Sammy points out that it survived cutting because it was hollow. Waist-high knees of this tree, still alive, spread out from the base of the tree and intermix with the rotting knees of trees that had been cut. Sammy changes direction, and we move again through the buttonbush, finally breaking through at the edge of a muddy pool with drying water lotus and pennywort. At the edge of the pool, dozens of nests made from dried sticks perch just above eye level in the buttonbush branches, abandoned this late in the year, but marking the location of an active rookery. Herons, cormorants, and egrets nested here, earlier in the year, when the water was higher.

To study amphibians, Sammy needs sites that he can reach at night, without wasting too much time hiking through thickets of buttonbush. "Ideally," he says, "I'd like to set up sampling clusters, so that we can hit four or five stations in a few hours. Otherwise, we'll spend all of our time moving between stations. We won't get enough data."

Back in the truck, we drive onto a paved road, then turn onto another road leading to Stutt's Field, and then leave the road to drive across Stutt's Field itself, over bean stubble. The site may be planted in trees as early as next year, and Sammy thinks it might be worth tracking amphibians as the field develops into forest.

The landscape dips, an expression of the broad arcs visible on the refuge map. "The swales are still obvious here," Sammy says. He stops to show me an impromptu drain formed by the ruts of tractor tires intentionally dug into the field to keep standing water away from crops. A rectangle of forest, privately owned and reputedly once hunted by Mickey Mantle, extends into the field, one of the missing pieces in the middle of the refuge. We look for a place where a swale runs from the field into the forest, so that we can see if there are obvious signs of the swales filling in, but most of the swales end within the field itself. The most likely candidate is off limits, on the private property that Mickey Mantle hunted.

"Most of the swales in the refuge are precip driven," Sammy says, meaning that they are flooded by rain—by precipitation. "I'd like to find some that are flooded with backwater from the river." There is an issue of water quality, especially in sites flooded by the Tensas River through low areas and channels, in what Sammy calls backwater flooding. The Tensas River has been called the most polluted river in the United States because of cotton pesticides that drain from its watershed, although it looks clean, just as Bayou Trepanier looked clean. Because amphibians are known to be sensitive to pollutants, it seems reasonable to suspect that there may be differences between the precipitation-driven swales and those driven by backwater flooding.

"There's an even bigger issue at stake here," Sammy says. "More and more people are linking what's happening up here with the dead zone in the Gulf. It's possible that these backwater swales could remove some of the pollutants, especially the nitrogen and phosphorus. This could be an impetus for even more restoration." The wetlands can convert nitrates in the water to gaseous forms of nitrogen that disperse from the water to the atmosphere, and phosphate can be sequestered in wetland sediments. Water coming into the swales, laden with nitrogen and phosphate from field runoff, could leave cleaner. But the same water could be loaded with cotton pesticides, and the ability of these swales to remove pesticides is unknown. It might be, too, that the isolated swales, the ones filled with rain water, especially those in forested lands that do not receive runoff from agricultural fields, could be islands of clean water, havens for sensitive amphibian species.

Without stopping, Sammy eats satsumas grown in the Louisiana Delta, probably in an impounded wetland, and a peanut butter sandwich. After lunch, we walk into the forest next to the field, moving fast along what appears to be a fire trail, developing a feel for the land. The trail moves up and down over ridges and into swales, with water oak, willow oak, and sweetgum on the ridges, and nuttall oak, overcup oak, and ash in the swales. But this is nothing like what we had seen earlier in the day. It has no cypress or buttonbush. Nothing here could be called a lake.

"This would look really different if it was wet," Sammy says.

We drive again, this time turning onto a dirt road that follows Judd Bayou through forest to a point where a fallen log blocks our path, then moving on by foot toward Judd Lake. Like Lake Nick, Judd Lake holds no water. The soil is cracked, and, in places, the dry clay floor of the lake has shrunk away from the roots of trees, leaving roots exposed. Dense patches of tall cutgrass block our progress, the serrate leaf edges tearing at our skin. Before we find standing water, well before we have fully explored the area for potential sites, we turn back.

I think again of Mark Davis's belief that every project should be part of a bigger picture. "It troubles me," I say, "that there is no clear link between the restoration up here and that on the coast." Sammy says nothing, but presses on, backtracking through dense cutgrass growing head-high and blocking our vision of the way out.

After dark but before dinner, I talk to Sammy in his hotel room, on the edge of Interstate 20, north of the Tensas National Wildlife Refuge. There is a sofa and a bed, but nowhere else to sit. I sit on the sofa and

Sammy sits on the bed while we talk. A photocopied article lies on the dresser, apparently something that Sammy is reading in preparation for a meeting in which he hopes to have some small influence on dam policy in east Texas. Sammy lives in hotels like this for perhaps one-quarter of each year, depending on his fieldwork load. He peels a satsuma and eats it while simultaneously unlacing and removing his boots.

"Engineers," he tells me, "talk about controlling water levels within a foot or so. But what we're talking about here is six inches or less. A difference of six inches could kill every tree in the forest." He tells me about the New Madrid earthquakes that hit Missouri with three massive shocks in 1811 and 1812, supposedly generated by drag on the westward-moving North American plate, far from the usual earthquake zones. Sammy has read work by Thomas Nuttall, a wandering naturalist and eccentric of the early nineteenth century, known among many other things for using the barrel of his gun as a digging stick. Nuttall's narrative describes the effect of the New Madrid quakes, including massive dieback of bottomland forests, drowned by a few inches of elevation change.

"Six inches," Sammy says, "could kill hundreds of acres of trees."

I tell him about Feyerabend's belief that scientists are advocates of ideas. He has not read Feyerabend, but he immediately understands. "The true grit," he says, "comes from reigning yourself in. If the data don't support your ideas, you need the strength to abandon the ideas." He pops a piece of satsuma into his mouth. "If your idea is wrong," he says, "you need to be able to admit it."

The conversation shifts from scientific advocacy to conservation advocacy. "In Louisiana," Sammy tells me, "we need people to stand up. They need to stand up as citizens of the state, and not necessarily as scientists. We've been hard on this state. I'm from Louisiana, and I'm not criticizing the state as an outsider. It's important for scientists to delineate between fact and opinion, but if a scientist feels strongly about something, he should speak up. If you're a scientist, you're still a citizen. You should be able to state your opinion, just like any citizen."

I suggest to him that scientists sometimes seem like tourists, looking at the world as if through the window of a tour bus, but remaining detached and uninvolved. He disagrees.

"In the natural resource fields," he says, "it's the controversial issues that draw scientists. People like Aldo Leopold were scientists but they were also involved with conservation. What you're saying, though, may be one of the differences between the natural resource fields and the more traditional life sciences—the difference between forestry or wildlife ecology on the one hand and botany or zoology on the other hand. I don't want to belabor this point, because I know people trained as botanists who are deeply involved with conservation, but it seems to me that the tradition of the more pure life sciences is one of detachment, while the tradition of the natural resource sciences is one of involvement."

Recently, Sammy had attended a National Research Council meeting in Washington, D.C. The meeting was by invitation only. There were government regulatory people, economists, and natural resource scientists like Sammy. The meeting's intent was to come to grips with the concepts of valuation—of what a forest is worth to society in dollar terms. But as the meeting progressed, it became apparent that it would be difficult to bridge the gap between science and policy, that even if the economists could come to grips with the vagaries of assigning values to commodities that are neither bought nor sold, and even if the resource scientists could list the services that different forests provide to society, it would make little difference in terms of policy. The meeting broke up with an expectation that the way forward would have to address the gap between science and policy. I recall commenting to Mark Davis that policy makers would not be able to ignore the fiscal importance of conservation if science could support the links between the environment and the economy. I see now, from Sammy's experience, that things may not be that simple.

"To me," I say, "that sounds incredibly discouraging."

"You have to keep things in perspective," Sammy says. "You have to remember that things are changing. When you and I were kids, no one would have dreamed of the kinds of gains that have been made through wetland restoration in the past twenty years. Almost no one would have thought of a meeting in Washington looking at the value of forests in terms of anything other than board feet of timber. It's a slow process, but we're moving forward. When we get knocked down, we just get back up. We say, 'Okay, that didn't work, so let's try something else.' But if we make a step forward, that's a step forward."

When I ask about concrete evidence of change that may have resulted from his own work, he refuses to take credit for anything. Instead, he says that his work has contributed to a larger movement. At stake is the forest, the dead zone, water quality for human health, economic health, extinctions. Holding the shredded peel of a satsuma in one hand, field boots lying next to his feet, in a hotel room well within earshot of Interstate 20, Sammy talks for a while about maintaining a passion for what he is doing, about moving past the setbacks and understanding that the contributions of an individual scientist form part of a voice that is, eventually, heard in Washington. His comments make me think of the words on the side of his truck: "Science for a changing world."

Living in the Bayou

In 1986, Denise Reed came to LUMCON, the Louisiana Universities Marine Consortium, in Cocodrie, Louisiana, at the edge of the Gulf. She came there from England, with a doctorate degree from Cambridge. In 1992, Hurricane Andrew struck. Andrew crossed southern Florida in less than six hours, leaving behind twenty-five billion dollars in damage, then swung north across the Gulf, toward Louisiana. As Andrew approached, Denise and her colleagues threw plastic sheets over equipment and books that could be damaged if the roof leaked. They packed computers into trucks and moved them to Denise's house, which sits on stilts eighteen miles inland from Cocodrie, in Montegut, a bayou town that could only appear as a safe haven in comparison to the edge of the Gulf itself. They moved the laboratory's airboat to Montegut, too, and tied it down in Denise's front yard.

By the time Andrew hit the Louisiana coast, he had grown to a Category IV storm; he carried a seven-foot storm surge and sustained winds blowing at 140 miles per hour. Before he reached the mainland, Andrew took out a third of Raccoon Island and the entire western arm of Whiskey Island—just removed them, erased them from the map. He came ashore near Cypremort Point, placing Cocodrie, and Denise's laboratory, near the storm's forward right quadrant—its strongest section, where the storm's forward momentum and its counterclockwise winds join forces. He flung pieces of soil and vegetation as large as cars from marshes into canals and onto the tops of levees. In places, he left behind accordion folds of land, like gopher mounds a yard wide and two feet tall, resulting from what Denise and her colleagues later called "lateral compression," alluding to Andrew's force against the shore, his ability to squash the land.[34]

Denise's home, protected as it was by miles of marsh, withstood Andrew. But after the storm, Denise drove to her laboratory behind a Red Cross truck. As the truck moved closer to Cocodrie, at the edge of the marsh, the Red Cross crew spent more and more time removing debris from the road—small things, but also downed trees and power poles, boats, parts of houses. As expected, the laboratory leaked. Where windows remained intact, the plastic sheets had protected equipment and boots. But on one side of the building, gravel blown from a tar-and-gravel roof had broken windows and Andrew had stormed through, an uninvited guest on a rampage. Most of the LUMCON crew was pressed into cleanup service, but Denise slipped away to check her work, in this case dozens of plastic plates scattered around the marsh to trap sediment. When she tells me about Andrew, it is not the storm's strength that she emphasizes, or the damage, or anxiety raised by the storm. Her emphasis is on Andrew as an opportunity to understand marsh processes, to see how Louisiana works.[35]

She no longer works at LUMCON, but she still lives in Montegut, and she still wants to learn more about how Louisiana works. She commutes over an hour from Montegut to her office and laboratory in the Department of Geology at the University of New Orleans, on the shore of Lake Pontchartrain. Because the Louisiana coast results from the extension and withdrawal of delta lobes that leave behind deep convolutions, she can drive from her home in one coastal environment, commute inland seventy miles, and park her car in another coastal environment, on the shores of Lake Pontchartrain.

"Living in the bayou gives me a special perspective on wetland loss," she tells me, "and on the way it affects people's lives—on what they think about it. It becomes more than just data." Her office was once a laboratory, and the sink and counter remain behind her desk, but bookshelves now cover one entire wall, holding books such as *The Hydraulic Behavior of Estuaries, Wildflowers,* ecology texts, and equipment catalogs. A table standing near the door seems to serve no other purpose than temporary storage for a constant two-way flow of printed material. Her office houses no Anglophilic memorabilia, nothing to suggest that she misses England. Her accent, though, remains strongly English, but clearly not the English of the House of Lords—somewhat closer to cockney, more down to earth, an accent that lobs off the hard sounds of *t* and *p* and occasionally discards whole syllables.

"Court reporters," she tells me, "have trouble with my accent. They ask me to repeat things. And in the bayou it's always been kind of a joke, the way I talk. Or people say they like it." She wears jeans, a blue sweat-shirt-style sweater, and white tennis shoes. At nine in the morning, she pours her third cup of coffee in a cup with a cartoon drawing of a hippopotamus and the slogan, inexplicably, "Go ahead, make my tea." It occurs to me that giving Denise Reed coffee may be akin to running a fan in a hurricane—the extra energy is just not needed.

"I've known your work for years," I tell her, "and my impression has been that you are an ecologist interested in sedimentation. But now I find you are a geologist."

"I'm a geomorphologist," she tells me. "Being a geomorphologist means understanding landscapes. And with marshes, you have to under-stand a little bit about plants. But I'm not an ecologist. I have cocktail party conversations about fish, but I don't have any conversations about invertebrates." She laughs when she tells me this, a raucous laugh, making me think of Don Cahoon. I remind her that she has published on fish in marshes, with Lawrence Rozas.[36] "Well, yes," she admits, "I like fish. I mean, I'm interested in fish. But I would never pretend to do fish work. I can't imagine me going out and actually sampling fish. I would harvest and weigh plants, maybe. That's more within my scope."

Among many papers that are soon to be published, on the publishing conveyor belt between her computer and the pages of scientific journals and academic books, Denise has an article on what she calls "coastal bio-geomorphology."

"It's about the interactions between plants and accretionary processes and the role of plants in forming creek networks," she says. "That sort of thing. Maybe you can see that as a kind of a theme in the things I've worked on—the relationship between the living and physical worlds. I've got other papers coming out now about the biotic dynamics of accretionary processes. Not in terms of plant dynamics, but about how plants interact with physical processes."

I ask her, as I have asked others, about the role of science in saving Louisiana. "Let's think about what we mean by science," she says. "Let's say that science is a sound technological understanding of the way things work. Does that sound like a reasonable definition? It's important to clarify that. We sometimes get in trouble with some of the agency environmental managers when we talk about 'scientists,' because many of them think of themselves as scientists. They have scientific training, but their mission in life is not to keep up with the literature and to do research, like ours is. Maybe we should talk about research science and research scientists. Research science has played a role in identifying the problems and understanding some of what causes land loss, even though there's still a great deal that we don't understand. We tend to gloss over what we don't know, because we know so much about land loss." She gestures broadly with her coffee cup—"Make my tea"—taking in the whole room, the whole state, in this statement. But then she leans forward, resting her elbows lightly on the desk and clasping the coffee cup, two-handed, in front of her. "We shouldn't forget about the things we don't know. In terms of actually solving the problem, though, we're still not basing restoration on the best available understanding of what needs to be done. There's been some improvement in the past few years, but we have a long way to go. One reason for that is the major bureaucracies that we've set up to select and implement projects. Another reason is that university researchers don't get involved with the process because we don't get any professional credit for it. And another reason is the time it takes for projects to actually get on the ground."

I tell her about Steve Faulkner's comment calling scientists just one more lobbying group. "The scientist," I say, "is in line with the oyster fisherman and the shrimp fisherman and the guy who's worried about flooding in his backyard, and the politicians are listening to all of it equally."

"Louisiana is more than just fish and plants," she replies. "Louisiana is a landscape with people in it, and the people have expectations. The reason we do this, the reason we go after money to restore Louisiana, is the people. It's not the bugs and bunnies. So you can't do it in isolation. What I'd like to see is restoration plans drawn up on the basis of the best available scientific information. Use that information, but don't ignore the socioeconomic situation. Far too frequently, you find university scientists operating independently of the socioeconomic landscape. They see the marsh as some eco-thing rather than as a resource. Part of that is because Baton Rouge is in Baton Rouge, it's not in Cocodrie. The scientists don't drive through the bayou every day. They don't live in the bayou. They're not people who are directly impacted by land loss. If a road floods, they read about it in the paper. They see it on the news. But they're not stranded."

Denise has been described to me as the scientific advisor for the Coalition to Restore Coastal Louisiana, the nonprofit advocacy group directed by Mark Davis. When I ask her what this means, she pauses for several seconds—the first noticeable pause in her responses, indicating, I think, that her role evolves over time, in response to the needs of the day and inconstant professional relationships. Then, instead of offering a general answer, she gives me an example. She will be running a meeting on freshwater diversions and the dead zone issue in the Gulf of Mexico, she tells me. The freshwater diversions are large structures that divert Mississippi River water through levees into areas where saltwater intrusion seems to impact marshes.[37] She means, specifically, the Caernarvon structure just downstream from New Orleans, the Davis Pond structure under construction twenty-four miles upstream from New Orleans, and a third structure planned near Norco, just west of New Orleans, at the Bonnet Carre spillway. The meeting will bring together fifteen scientists, by invitation only, in an attempt to find a consensus about what Mississippi River water is doing to the Gulf and, by extension, about the wisdom of diverting Mississippi River water into productive estuaries. The consensus she hopes for is not entirely one on the details of what is happening, but rather one on the state of the scientific understanding, a consensus that separates opinion from data, that separates personal viewpoints from what approaches scientific fact.

"This is a very divisive issue," she says. "People are polarized on this. I said that I'm running the meeting, but that's not right. I'm facilitating. I'm organizing. I don't actually know much about this issue on a technical level. It's not my field. But I know the people who do know something. This is a way that I can help the Coalition on something that they should be working on. The Coalition is the right organization to host this meeting."

I suggest to Denise that her work—her research focus—differs from that of many others in that it looks at sediment deposition in detail. Others are satisfied with a vision of water spreading across a marsh and dropping its sediment load along the way, but Denise wants to know more. She

The Davis Pond freshwater diversion structure under construction

looks at different sediment grain sizes, organic versus inorganic sediments, spatial patterns, seasonal differences, the influence of storms. She nods at my description. "Storms and levees," she says. "The effects of storms and levees on sediment deposition patterns. Those are the things that I like to think I've made a contribution in. My cold-front paper—did you read my cold-front paper?"

She says that the three papers that please her most—in the sense of self-assessment, in the sense of someone with the presence of mind to step back and reflect on her own work, to see its strengths and weaknesses, to recognize what is more valuable and what is less valuable—are her cold-front paper, her paper on marsh survival and submergence, and her paper on sediment deposition and marsh management.[38] She is quantitative even here, counting the papers off with raised fingers: one, two, three. It is part of her character to quantify, to count, to measure, to be precise, to consider the data numerically. But this part of her personality is counterbalanced by her understanding of Louisiana as a landscape with people, by the reality of living in the bayou.

Her voice, talking about marsh management and sediment deposition, was one of several that dramatically slowed the use of impoundments and weirs as restoration tools in south Louisiana. The levee-weir combination, nothing more than a set of levees surrounding a marsh with wooden weirs to control water levels, had been used to manage marshes since before Denise was born. This approach to water-level management was once described in terms of providing habitat for ducks and in terms of holding enough water on a marsh to float a pirogue or a johnboat. The levee-weir combination brought in the birds, then ensured the presence of enough water to give hunters access. Later, a shift occurred. People began thinking of the levee-weir combination as a means of protecting the marsh, of preventing saltwater intrusion and subsidence, of restoring disappearing marshes. The levee-weir combination came to be known as "structural marsh management," or SMM, in the lexicon of natural resource management. But as a widely known secret, something that did not appear in the literature but was often discussed at hunting camps, landowners perceived that leveed marsh remains the property of the landowner even if it subsides to become open water, while unleveed marsh, once it subsides to become open water, belongs to the state. By the 1990s, landowners and managers motivated by concerns over bird habitat, marsh preservation, and legal protection used the levee-weir combination to manage an area equivalent in size to a five-mile strip stretching from Baton Rouge to the Texas border. It was in this setting of massive and well-intentioned land management that Denise and her colleagues voiced their concerns about the efficacy of the levee-weir combination.

"I hope," Denise says, in reference to her investigations of sediment deposition in impoundments, "that my work helped put to bed an issue that had been dogging us for a long while—at least here in the Delta. What is happening on the Chenier Plain may be a whole different story." The work she refers to involved sediment trapping in four study sites, each divided between impounded and unimpounded areas. She used aluminum wire to pin sediment traps, fashioned from plastic dishes and filter paper, to the marsh surface in the study sites, waited two weeks, then retrieved the filter paper, dried it, and weighed the trapped sediment. The impoundments that were built as part of this study enclosed something like nine hundred acres. To access her traps, she and her colleagues built forty boardwalks, with a combined length of one-third of a mile. From the boardwalks, she could work without disturbing the marsh surface. Much like a Cajun trapper working a trapline for muskrat or nutria, she returned to each boardwalk again and again, every two weeks, for four years. At the end of four years, she had nineteen thousand samples, all contributing to her understanding of how Louisiana works and leading to the final sentence of an eleven-page paper: "If managers wish to maintain marsh conditions within existing impoundments, they should re-examine their existing strategies of water-level manipulations and seek new approaches to marsh management."[39]

"There are natural processes that move sediments around," she says, leaning back in her chair, "and levees get in the way. I believe that those two things are inherently encompassed in our most recent planning for Louisiana. Now, in our plans, you do not see levees all across the place. You see a system that is open and you see a system that allows material to move around. The approach you might have seen before in Louisiana was a controlled system, right? Now the approach is much more of a self-sustaining system. I'm not taking any kind of credit for that, but it has been a kind of progress in thinking that my work may have contributed to. Look at the CWPPRA restoration plan from 1993. It called for lots of little projects that built levees around marshes and tried to control water movement. Now we don't want to control things, we want to manage them."

She talks about the complexities of sediment deposition and about moving beyond the belief that simply supplying sediment to subsided areas is enough. Her work looks at sediment deposition, which is distinct from accretion, which is distinct from elevation change. If sediment that is deposited stays on location—if it is not resuspended and moved elsewhere—it contributes to accretion. Elevation change is the difference between accretion and subsidence. "They should know now that you need a sediment outfall plan," she says, referring to managers and engineers. "If all you do is deliver the sediment, it goes where it wants to, it moves around the way it wants to, and that may not be where you need it. It's not just a matter of poking a hole in the levee to let sediment flow through. You need a plan."

Denise's work became a nail in the coffin for structural marsh management as a restoration tool in southeastern Louisiana, but it was only one of many nails. "There were others looking at the effects of marsh management," she says, "Irv Mendelssohn, Don Cahoon, lots of others besides me. Don Cahoon still goes red in the face over impoundments. EPA tried to grab the issue of structural marsh management. They tried to develop guidelines for policy makers on judging marsh-management permit applications.[40] They tried to clarify the issues by developing guidelines. In the end, people stopped using them for restoration, at least in southeast Louisiana."

From one of Denise's most recent publications, written in collaboration with scientists from Louisiana State University, I read a passage suggesting that research into structural marsh management "could have far-reaching implications for the protection and management of saline wetlands nationwide."[41] Then I explain to her that many of the wetland scientists I have spoken to in Louisiana expressed disappointment over the disjunction between science and management, over what they see as a fissure separating scientists and policy makers and a tendency for scientists to talk among themselves.

She leans back in her chair, tilts her head slightly to one side, and raises her eyebrows in surprise.

Although I had known Denise's work for several years, we met in person for the first time only a few months before, at the Estuarine Research Federation's conference in New Orleans, a forum for the exchange of ideas about the science of estuarine systems. Denise was one of the conference's key organizers. "It's like throwing a party for three hundred of your best friends and having an extra five hundred show up," she told me at the time. During the session held to discuss the possibility of somehow aligning the Estuarine Research Federation and Restore America's Estuaries, Denise described the importance of forming personal relationships. She suggested that scientists needed to build trust with managers, with policy makers, with agency personnel. In the row in front of me, a man leaned over to the woman sitting next to him and, in a voice barely loud enough for me to hear, said, "The good-ol'-boy network in Louisiana—that's how it works down here."

Now, riding east from the University of New Orleans toward the Caernarvon Freshwater Diversion Structure in Denise's car, I bring this up, reluctantly, afraid that I might insult her. But she is not insulted. Instead, she seems to see this as an interesting idea, worth considering. But she does not believe that anyone has tried to influence her thinking, to talk her into something that did not come from her data. She relates a story about research funded by a private company. The research effectively stopped the company from moving ahead with what could have been a financially valuable project, and, although the company discontinued her research funding, the conflict, by Denise's self-assessment, had no influence on interpretation of the data. The good-ol'-boy network, if it existed at all, broke down here, bogged by the data, or by a British immigrant to the bayou who lacked the background to understand how it was supposed to work, or, most likely, by the unconscious and automatic application of scientific integrity and strength of character, prerequisites for wetland scientists working in Louisiana.

It is the day after the Sugar Bowl, but traffic, even through the suburbs of New Orleans, is surprisingly light. We head generally southeast, following the roads in a zigzag course that roughly parallels a Mississippi River meander sweeping past New Orleans, flowing east, then bending south, then swinging west again at the community of Caernarvon, our planned destination, fifteen miles downstream from New Orleans. The route takes us through urban sprawl, across canals, along a levee. In traffic, we pass a pickup so overloaded with celery that it rests on its back shocks. The celery, almost certainly, was harvested from a drained wetland. We go to Caernarvon not to see the community, but to see the structure known officially as the Caernarvon Freshwater Diversion Structure, but typically referred to simply as Caernarvon, commandeering the community's name while at the same time putting it on the map, lending the community an importance that it might not otherwise have.

In a wandering conversation, I ask Denise about removing the Old River Control Structure. "This is something I'm asking everyone I talk to," I tell her. Like all of the others, she prefaces her answer by saying that removal of the Old River Control Structure is not a realistic option.

"If we could remove the Old River Control Structure," she says, "would it really solve our problems? Suppose we could let the Atchafalaya capture the Mississippi River and just forget about the problems it would cause for New Orleans and Baton Rouge? Or suppose we could manage the Old River Structure to build more wetlands? Maybe we would get more wetlands in the Atchafalaya Delta. We might even gain enough wetland acreage to counterbalance losses elsewhere. Would that be okay? We would still have a problem in Barataria Bay. Would it be okay to let the Barataria Bay wetlands disappear completely? We're managing for people here. This is a landscape of people."

As a person who spends a great deal of her time in meetings, trying to bring a scientist's perspective to the management of Louisiana, as the scientific advisor to the Coalition to Restore Coastal Louisiana, as a person who lives in the bayou, a theme of her thoughts, one that moves beyond the science of sediment movement, considers the landscape of people, of human lives and livelihoods. It moves toward restoration as good business, as good politics, as good socioeconomic practice. It moves beyond Denise's coastal biogeomorphology to something that might one day be called coastal sociobiogeomorphology or, better, coastal anthrobiogeomorphology.

"There's a paradigm out there for fisheries," she says. "There's this paradigm that looks at delta building and delta degradation, and we say that degrading marshes are good for fisheries. Fish like subsiding marshes. Fisheries are improved on the degradation side of the curve because fish get edge habitat and access to more areas as the marsh breaks up. And the marsh is low so that it floods more often. Things like that, right? So this paradigm says that the only way you can restore fish habitat in Louisiana is by building land and then letting it deteriorate, until you get the productivity that goes along with subsiding marshes. That's the kind of paradigm that's out there based on natural cycles."

With one hand on the steering wheel and one hand gesturing, describing curves of delta building and degradation, emphasizing points, we turn from one road to another without pause.

"So if we extend this to restoration," she says, "we build a crevasse, say, and we build land, then wait for it to deteriorate until we get the productivity. And on the larger scale, then, people think that we have to build and let it degrade—this whole idea of a pulsing paradigm, where we build land in one area and let the land degrade in another, so that we are using the natural cycle to our advantage—managing it. But that is not an appropriate restoration paradigm. We need to circumvent that loop, right? In restoration approaches we need to develop self-maintaining systems that are not degrading but that are maintaining at a certain level of productivity."

"You're looking toward a more managed system," I suggest. "A more engineered system?"

"It's already an engineered system," she says. "We're really not talking about a natural ecosystem here in Louisiana. We need to use engineering to our advantage. The first thing we need to do is identify the attributes of the landscape that interest us. What is our goal landscape? What are its attributes? The landscape has a certain pattern to it. It has a certain biodiversity to it. It has gradients. We have to develop an understanding of these attributes, then restore to maintain that landscape—maybe by using freshwater diversion structures, but using that kind of engineering in a way to maintain the goal landscape. Maybe that means managing diversion structures in a particular way for decades at a time, or maybe only allowing them to flow in the spring or only during certain years. And that's where 'restore' is the wrong word. We're really talking about management. We're talking about moving away from a paradigm of restoration to one of management. We're not making something into what it once was. What we are doing is maintaining the system as what we want."

What the system was—a constantly changing environment, on time scales that make a difference to humans, on time scales that can affect a thirty-year mortgage or a fifty-year business plan—is no longer acceptable. Denise's thesis is that we need to manage the system. And to do that, we need a consensus on management objectives, and we need the knowledge to move toward those objectives. What do we want and how can we get it?

With Denise, frank statements displace British diplomacy. In this she is more American than most Americans. "I don't agree with Gene Turner on some things," she says. "We get along well, but I don't agree with him about small projects. His ideas about small projects won't work. The scale is all wrong. Sure, crevasse splays are a good thing. Backfilling canals is okay, too, to a point. But these are just small projects on a huge landscape. And they only focus on one goal—replacement of lost acreage. And that may not be the right goal."

I ask if she thinks that disagreements among scientists hurt their ability to influence management and policy. "Only when managers and policy makers don't understand science," she answers. "If they understand, they know that disagreement is part of the process."

In talking about disagreements among scientists, she uses the phrase "outstanding issues," referring to those issues that are not black-and-white, that go beyond available data. " 'Outstanding issues'—that's a great euphemism," I say, thinking of people who will not speak to certain colleagues, who might think twice, on their most vindictive days, before throwing a life preserver to a drowning colleague.

Just past the community of Caernarvon, we turn left onto a short stretch of gravel, cross railroad tracks, and park. We get out of the car and walk up to the structure. It is concrete, fenced in, unmanned. It is capable of moving sixty thousand gallons of Mississippi River water into Breton Sound every second. The water moves through five box culverts, each one measuring 15 feet by 15 feet. Iron lift gates, fifty-seven thousand pounds each, control flow through the culverts. The intakes stretch along 175 feet of the Mississippi River's bank, and water flowing through the structure passes into a one-and-one-half-mile-long canal before discharging into Breton Sound, itself fifty miles long and twenty miles wide, attached, at its far end, to the Gulf of Mexico. Next to a river that has become a marvel of engineering through a century of levee construction, dredging, channelization, and damming, the Caernarvon Freshwater Diversion Structure is yet another engineering coup, proof that almost anything can be built: its construction required rerouting of roads and railroad tracks, erection of a temporary dam into the Mississippi River surrounding the site of Caernarvon's intakes, pumps to dewater the construction site, driving of 850 concrete piles, manufacture of massive lift gates to specifications that ensured a seal tight enough to hold water.

Caernarvon immediately reminds me of the Old River Control Structure, but the purpose here, at Caernarvon, is one of restoration, not flood control. To be clear, though, restoration in the context of Caernarvon means restoration of low salinity levels in Breton Sound, downstream from Caernarvon's discharge; it does not mean restoration of sediment flow. Caernarvon is not a giant crevasse splay project. The structure was not designed to pass sediment, and most of the sediment that finds its way through the structure settles out in Big Mar, a basin between Breton Sound and the structure itself, in-line with Caernarvon's discharge canal. Sediment, while required to build marsh, kills oysters, and preservation of the oyster fishery was, in part, what drove construction of Caernarvon.

Arguably, salinization of Breton Sound reflected natural evolution in a subsiding delta lobe cut off from its sediment source. Equally arguably, salinization reflected changes brought about in the name of navigation and flood control improvements. The cause, though, was irrelevant. People were accustomed to a Breton Sound with low salinities; they were dependent on it. From at least the 1960s, they worried about salinization. In 1965, only three years after the Old River Control Structure began operating, the Flood Control Act authorized the Caernarvon project, an engineering solution to an ecological problem during a time when ecology as a discipline was only beginning to find its feet. In the sense that it might return Breton Sound to the lower salinities of past days, Caernarvon targeted a restoration goal. But really, it was a form of what Denise had earlier described as management. It targeted a self-maintaining system with a certain level of productivity, a system that by-passed or totally ignored the natural cycles of deltaic birth and death.

Although the Flood Control Act authorized Caernarvon in 1965, construction required twenty-six million dollars, an amount that awaited the Water Resources Development Act of 1986. Planning and design took two more years, and construction itself took three years. Water flowed through the five fifteen-by-fifteen-foot box culverts for the first time in 1991, almost thirty years after its conception.

Earlier, in her office, Denise had suggested that one reason for the poor link between restoration and science, in the sense of science as sound technology, was the long time required to get projects in the ground. The science could change between the time of project conception and project completion. I ask her if that could be the case here, given the changes in thinking between 1965, when Caernarvon was conceived, and 1986, when Caernarvon was designed. Instead of answering, she hands me a packet of twelve photocopied pages, something she had used in a lecture, opened now to a list of Caernarvon discharge rates planned for each month.

"Caernarvon was designed for about eight thousand cubic feet per second," she says. "But at peak discharge, it's managed at three to four thousand cubic feet per second. For most months discharge rates are even lower. They decreased discharge rates because of concerns about erosion and marsh loss. But I challenge that. I don't know that they have an erosion problem that can't be dealt with. And those are planned discharge rates. Right now the river is low, so the gates are closed altogether. We're in January, and it should be flowing at three or four thousand cubic feet per second, but it's not flowing at all."

I think, for a moment, of who "they" might be. I envision an engineer in a cubicle somewhere in New Orleans, beleaguered by opinions, uncertain of what to do not because of incompetence, but because he or she is navigating unexplored waters. The only sure thing is that any action, including the do-nothing option of no action at all, will attract criticism.

Among Denise's twelve pages of handouts are graphs plotting catches of seed and sack oysters, of brown shrimp, of white shrimp. The numbers for brown and white shrimp show no clear pattern, nothing beyond year-to-year changes, the good years and bad years of fishing. But seed and sack oysters soared beginning in 1991, increasing from fewer than half a million before 1991 to more than one million in 1992. For three years beginning in 1994, counts brushed close to five million—more than a tenfold increase. Counts of muskrat houses, too, increased more than tenfold after 1991. These changes—for the engineer in a New Orleans cubicle, for the oystermen in Breton Sound, for the politicians who turned on the flow of money that turned on the flow of water through Caernarvon—could only spell success.

"The goals of the project," Denise says, "were enhancement of marsh growth and reduced marsh loss as well as increased fisheries and wildlife productivity. For a time, some people claimed that there had been a gain of several hundred acres in marsh area. But when we wanted to know more about the data, they backed away from that claim. I don't think anyone is making that claim for the whole project area anymore. The main intent of Caernarvon was always reduced salinity, not land gain. And knowing what we now know about the need for sediment input to sustain marshes, it's not surprising that Caernarvon has not been really successful in increasing the area of marsh."

I tell her that I have seen in Louisiana many projects that claim to be successful when there is little evidence of success. "The terraces in Calcasieu Lake are an example," I say. "One of the selling points was to trap sediment and build land, but now people talk about them in terms of providing edge habitat for fish. It's been a change in focus. I wonder if we are playing musical objectives? It's a kind of revisionist history that might prevent us from learning from mistakes. For Caernarvon, do you think that flow rates of less than half the design rate are an admission of failure? Or at least an admission of over-designing?"

She tells me that sediment trapping was only one of the goals of the terracing at Calcasieu Lake and that while it failed to trap sediment it has met some of its other goals. Then she says that she sees Caernarvon as good for marsh maintenance, if not for building or rebuilding marsh. "It is not an issue of flawed thinking," she says. "Diversions are fundamentally sound. The design can be improved, but the principle is sound." Caernarvon reconnects the river with its marshes. It provides freshwater and nutrients. Even though Caernarvon may not be designed to pass sediments, fine sediments suspended in the water find their way through.

"Caernarvon may have taught us that we need lots of small taps all up and down the levee rather than one big tap," she says, "but I think the powers that be are happy with the structure. I don't know that anyone would back away from what has been done out here. Management of flows below capacity is a good thing. It's a sign that we can adapt our practices as we acquire more information. And there has been talk of dredging the discharge channel to accommodate sediment flows, now that we recognize how important sediment flow really is. There has even been talk of agitation dredging at the structure intake to stir up sediment that can flow through the structure. And, of course, that's not what this was designed for. There's been talk of a lawsuit calling for more flow to the south. We learn as we go. That's the important thing. But no one talks about backing out of Caernarvon. No one thinks of it as a failure."

From Caernarvon, we head east, away from the river, and then south, toward Delacroix, to see if we can get out onto the marsh itself. We pass through a hurricane wall—a trip wire for storm surges moving inland. We pass a school on stilts. The road stands above the surrounding ground, built on material dug from a long, flooded ditch that parallels the road itself. Both road and ditch play a role in the replumbing of Louisiana, the road as a dam that blocks flows and the ditch as a conduit that moves water. A kingfisher flies from its perch in a transformer station, skipping in punctuated bursts across the sky in front of Denise's car. A hawk sits on a power line, staring out over the marsh.

The marsh on the way to Delacroix, in relative terms, is an area of low subsidence. Denise wonders aloud about a stand of dead trees. "Usually dead trees are a sign of subsidence," she says. "The ground sinks far enough to kill the trees. But it can also be a sign of salinization or impoundment. Dead cypress are a good sign of salinization because they can tolerate flooding but they can't tolerate salt. Dead oak trees signify flooding, because they can't handle the water. Maybe someone built something out here that let the saltwater in, or that holds freshwater when it rains." I think of plumbers with bulldozers replumbing Louisiana, but with no master plan and no blueprints.

To the right, across flat miles of mixed land and water, I can see New Orleans rising above the marsh, a wetter version of Las Vegas rising above the desert. In fact, though, it is a city beneath the marsh, kept dry by levees and pumps, by dam builders and plumbers, no different—aside from its blues clubs and restaurants and hotels and neighborhoods—than other impoundments in the marsh that, cut off from a source of sediment, subside.

Delacroix itself, a linear town built on high ground next to the bayou, is surprisingly prosperous. Fishing boats float at docks in front of well-kept homes, part of what Denise had earlier called a landscape with people, part of the reason that scientists may be seen as just one more lobbying group. The people here benefit from Caernarvon, ten miles across the marsh to the northwest. But there is nowhere convenient to access the marsh without wading through deep water or crossing through someone's yard. At the end of the road, we turn around and head back to New Orleans.

I ask Denise what she would change, right now, about the way restoration is approached in Louisiana. "I'd like to see the agencies involved with restoration proactively supporting research," she says. "I don't necessarily mean they should issue research grants, but it would be helpful if they could just be more supportive. A letter of support from someone highly placed with a state or federal agency could be really useful, but it's hard to get. And I'm frustrated by the view of spending down here as a pork barrel issue. When Louisiana gets federal dollars for wetlands, everyone talks about pork barrel spending, but no one worries about pork barrel spending when California gets money to protect and restore habitat for endangered fish. Would we be better off if we focused on endangered species?"

In her office at the University of New Orleans, telephone messages await Denise and new papers have appeared on the table next to her door. The workday has not ended. Before I leave Denise to her duties, she gives me a photocopied document awkwardly entitled *"Michael X. St. Martin & Virginia Rayne St. Martin versus Mobil Exploration & Producing U.S., Inc., et al., Partial Findings and Conclusions."*[42] I sit on a bench within sight of Lake Pontchartrain to read through the document's twenty-eight pages. In essence, it describes a lawsuit over lost land—a marsh suit heard by the United States District Court's Judge Marcel Livaudais. The plaintiffs believed that canals built by the defendants had led to erosion and the loss or damage of 357 acres of marsh habitat. They asked for restoration of the marsh, at an estimated cost of $39,000 an acre, or just shy of $14 million.

Expert witnesses from Louisiana State University testified for both sides. Defendants claimed that most of the land loss was from subsidence. The plaintiffs claimed that the deleterious effect of canals on coastal marsh loss was beyond dispute. An expert witness for the defendant argued that natural processes accounted for 71 percent of the land loss—not 70 percent or 72 percent, but 71 percent. Another expert witness talked about the complexity of land loss, about multiple causes acting synergistically. He suggested that grazing by nutria may have caused part of the problem, then admitted that this suggestion was based only on reading about nutria, rather than on personal observations of nutria. A witness for the plaintiff testified that he had studied nutria all along the Louisiana coast for forty years and that nutria had not caused land loss on the plaintiff's property.

In the end, Judge Livaudais decided that the expert witnesses were not, in the judge's own words, "very helpful." The scientists were, in this sense, more disputatious than coherent, just another lobbying group wrestling with what Denise had called outstanding issues. Judge Livaudais turned for guidance to *Roman Catholic Church v. Louisiana Gas Service Co.*, a 1993 case ruled on by the Louisiana Supreme Court, a case unrelated to wetlands.[43] The Louisiana Supreme Court decided that restoration payments exceeding the actual value of the land in question would be unreasonable. Upon reading this, it occurs to me that almost none of Louisiana's restoration plans would pass this test. But Judge Livaudais, after hearing hours of testimony from the state's leading experts on wetland loss, considered that the plaintiffs had paid $245 an acre for their land and balanced this against restoration costs of $39,000 an acre. He ruled in favor of the plaintiffs, but only awarded $240,000 in damages— less than 2 percent of the plaintiff's requested figure.

By the time I finish reading, I feel certain that Denise is halfway home, back to a place where land loss is more than just a concept, to a landscape of people, to where the fact that scientists are just another lobbying group makes perfect sense.

Contaminated Paradise

In his day job, Senator Mike Robichaux works from an office wedged between Highway 1 and Bayou Lafourche in Raceland, Louisiana, eighty miles south of the capitol in Baton Rouge and, as the great blue heron flies, some sixteen miles from Denise Reed's home in Montegut. The office, a brick building with green shutters, sits next to a rundown boathouse built by his father. In front of the office is the shingle that pays the bills: a wooden sign proclaiming, "Mike Robichaux, MD, Ear Nose & Throat." Behind the office, Bayou Lafourche passes water, and to a lesser extent sediment, to the Gulf. Here, Bayou Lafourche is not much wider than Highway 1. Duckweed stretches out from both banks to cover two-thirds of the bayou's width, and the center third, clear of duckweed, reflects trees that grow from the bayou's steep banks. Fifty-five miles down this bayou, past Larose and Golden Meadow and Port Fourchon, Bayou Lafourche flows quietly into the Gulf. For most of those fifty-five miles, people live in homes built along both sides of the bayou, on high ground comprised of sediments deposited during floods long before they were born. Some of these people are Houma Indians. Some of them speak only an archaic dialect of French, largely intact from the days before the Louisiana Purchase. Mike's family has roots in Raceland. Like Mike himself, his father was a doctor, but his father was also an elected coroner.

Like Mike himself, his grandfather served as a state senator. It is important to know these things, because they establish this place as a part of Mike and Mike as a part of this place, inseparable from this landscape of people.

Mike lives across Highway 1 from his office, in a home built by his father. Despite Mike's status as a senator and a physician, the house, although large and well kept, does not register on the pretension scale. Along the driveway, wires extend upward from concrete stanchions, apparently awaiting an electrician to install lights. Wagons and tricycles lie scattered around the grounds like flood debris. Through the open garage door, I see a weight bench and a drum set. Barefooted, in shorts and a white undershirt, Mike escorts me to the kitchen. His hair is a respectable gray befitting of both politics and medicine. His eyes are brilliant blue. In the evening, when we meet for the first time, I thank him for seeing me, knowing that he has spent the day with patients across the street. In the accent of an educated Cajun, he tells me that it has been an easy day—he is normally up by four each morning, but today he slept in, until six. Now, he is halfway through a dinner of cheese-flavored corn chips.

Mike sits perched on the edge of a chair that squeaks every time he moves. Leaning forward, with his arms resting on the table, he describes his district. "There's no question," he says, "that this is a paradise. The Terrebonne-Barataria estuary is probably the most productive estuarine complex in the world. We have a shrimping industry that's just extraordinarily active. Everything out here is deltaic soil. You throw something in the ground and it grows. We've got a big sugar cane industry over here. We've got oil wealth—with three-dimensional seismography there's still some of that wealth left to be found. We've got industrial infrastructure as you move higher up into some of the bayous. We've got a wealth of culture. We've got people with a good work ethic. It's a cornucopia of very good things and it's a good quality of life. It's the dream of Louisiana."

He leans back, chair squeaking, and crosses his arms. "The downside is that we're poor in spite of all these resources. The state is poor. Last time I checked, per capita income in the United States was about $26,000 a year. Per capita income in Louisiana was twenty-one or twenty-two thousand. In our district, per capita income is $17,500. Education is poor.

Until 1964, Native Americans in this district couldn't go past seventh grade. That was by design. Their land was taken from them, and the land yielded unbelievable wealth, so it was convenient to keep them uneducated."

Bayou Lafourche had carried the Mississippi River until the Mississippi River swung to the east, to its current location, some seven hundred years ago. Because Mike's district hosts the youngest fully abandoned deltaic lobe, it is disappearing more quickly than many other parts of Louisiana. Recently deposited Mississippi River sediment subsides rapidly under its own weight, and without deposition of new sediment the tendency is for land to become water. Add to this a network of navigation and irrigation canals that change hydrology. Add to this sum the practice of impounding and pumping for agriculture. The result is clear: As much or more so than elsewhere in the state, the bottom is falling out of Senator Mike Robichaux's district. Stay here long enough, and you will need hip waders to walk to the polling booth.

"The thing you have to understand about land loss in Louisiana," Mike says, "is that it's part of a natural cycle. Louisiana loses about thirty-five square miles of land every year, and the bulk of that is right here in this district. The big killer is not the oil-field canals. They account for about a third of the losses, but most of it is just the soil disappearing."

"You say that as though it's a fact," I say. "You're confident that it's a third?"

"The experts say it's a third. I don't have any way to know other than what they say."

Mike does not believe that his training as a medical doctor, his education in the sciences, has given him an advantage in understanding wetland loss and restoration. But he maintains a small library on wetlands. His notes, compiled while reading through that library, exceed two hundred pages.

He leans forward again, reaching for a corn chip, then offering the bag to me. "We're in a drought right now," he says. "What we're going to see when the drought ends is that the land is lower. Low areas full of rainwater will be bigger. They'll stay wet longer. We'll be able to see that."

"Subsidence is noticeable over a year or two?" I ask.

"It's definitely noticeable. You can see the roots of trees exposed. This is organic soil. It just disappears when it dries out. You can look at areas that are leveed and drained. I'm thinking of Delta Farms. They did a wonderful job with the levees, a very appropriate job. But after they levee the land and pump it, it sinks even quicker than the land around it. Inside the levees, cypress stumps are popping up out of the soil. They haven't seen the light of day in hundreds of years, but the soil is just disappearing around them."

I ask about restoration in his district.

"Restoration efforts are miniscule compared to the magnitude of lost land," he says. "If everything works—if we took all of the CWPPRA plans and all of them worked—we would slow down losses by about 10 or 15 percent. We would not gain land." He pauses to consider this for a moment. "We have not become focused enough to get the job done at this time," he adds.

He talks about barrier island restoration, currently an important component of CWPPRA schemes. The barrier islands protect marshes from wave-driven erosion. East Timbalier Island, really more of a spit than an island, juts out near the mouth of Bayou Lafourche and runs east and west along the coastline. It protects Timbalier Bay and its marshes from the full onslaught of Gulf of Mexico winds and waves. "Barrier islands weren't even on the map in the early days of CWPPRA," Mike tells me. "They were below the CWPPRA radar."

It was the people of Mike's district, among others, who took the high ground in relation to barrier islands. In 1999, CWPPRA placed rock barriers along the shoreline of East Timbalier Island and pumped sand to increase the island's size and height and, according to a CWPPRA document, to "increase the island's life expectancy beyond the present estimate of eleven years."

He tells me about the Bayou Lafourche siphon, a project that CWPPRA considered but did not pursue. The siphon—a series of short pipelines that would cross the levee to join Bayou Lafourche and the Mississippi River—would have diverted Mississippi River water and sediment into

Bayou Lafourche at Donaldsville, where a flood protection dam had separated the river and the bayou in 1904. One plan called for flows of a
thousand cubic feet per second, a flow comparable to that of the Caernarvon diversion. Mike believes that the siphon project stalled because lobbyists had pushed for a different project at another location. "We can't do it
all," he says. "We have to decide what we want to protect and what we
don't want to protect."

I ask about the role of science in the decision-making process.

"When I started with this years ago, people were fussing about doing
studies," Mike says. "Lots of people said, 'We don't need more studies,
we need action.' Well, we did need the studies. But now we need action.
If we don't harness the Mississippi River, if we don't take the great wealth
of topsoil that we're throwing over the continental shelf right now and
use it to protect our wetlands, the whole southern part of this state will be
lost—not just my district. One good storm could take it all. New Orleans
will be wiped out."

He believes in a project that would pump sediment from the Mississippi River to the places where it is needed most, through a long pipeline,
much longer than those used in siphon projects. What he describes sounds
to me like a massively scaled-up version of dredged-material wetland creation, the kind of thing Steve Faulkner had shown me in the Atchafalaya
Delta, the kind of thing that had been done at Bayou LaBranche, near
where I had stood on the edge of Lake Pontchartrain with Mark Davis,
but all done on a grander scale, with sediment moving through a hundred
miles of permanent pipeline, adding a sediment spur line to the replumbing of Louisiana. The pipeline he envisions would run down the middle
of Bayou Lafourche, thereby avoiding right-of-way problems all the way
to the coast. A manifold at the end of the pipeline would send sediment
to areas with the greatest need. The project would, among other things,
protect Highway 1, the main thoroughfare—the only thoroughfare—to
Port Fourchon on the coast. An eight-inch pipeline, he believes, could
move more sediment than the whole of Bayou Lafourche. The expertise is
here—people in Louisiana, more so than anyone else, know how to lay
pipe. But this is not a project under official CWPPRA consideration.

"There's a time to cut bait," Mike says, "and a time to fish. It's time to fish. Let's get past these small projects and do something big, something that's going to make a difference, something with proven technology. And I don't know if this is it. I know some of the catchy terms, but I'm not a wetland scientist. I don't know if the pipeline idea will work. But let's get some big projects on the table." He pauses, then coughs to clear his throat. "The other big projects," he adds, "the big freshwater diversions, they seem to be working, but they're slow."

Thinking of Gene Turner and several others, I remark that not everyone believes the big diversions—Caernarvon and Davis Pond—will restore wetlands. Mike's eyes dart toward me in interest, and his eyebrows rise slightly, but he does not pursue the topic.

"If I could focus on wetlands entirely," he says, "I'd be jumping up and down, saying, 'Okay, here's what we should do.' I don't see anyone talking about this, but we know we can build land by pumping sediment. We know how to pump sediment through pipelines. Coal miners move coal slurry hundreds of miles through pipelines. If this turns out to be a bad idea, we can shoot it down and replace it with something else. Maybe it's too expensive. Maybe it's pie in the sky. But the first time someone brought up barrier island restoration, I thought that was pie in the sky, and now it's something that we're going after in a big way. Let's look at this and see if it's feasible. We need to think big."

As he talks, I remember my flight with Gene Turner. We had flown over Mike's district. We had flown over Delta Farms. The restoration projects I had seen were Band-Aids for cancer. But I think, too, of Gene's warnings: big projects bring big risks—risks of failure, of overspending, of worsening already bad environmental degradation.

I tell Mike that I see a parallel between medical science and wetland science, in that both fields present information that affects the public and that both fields have shifted their positions or experienced disagreement within their ranks regarding key points. I read to him from an Associated Press article that explains why the medical profession has pulled back on its anti-egg and anti-salt positions, why it seems to vacillate in its advice. According to the article, which quotes Dr. Walter Willet of the Harvard

School of Public Health, physicians make strong claims based on weak data. They go out on a limb, presenting certain positions as factual when in fact they are not well established. It is one of the reasons that people have begun to lose faith in their doctors.

"We've got good, competent people studying our wetlands," Mike comments. "The science is good, but it's not always in harmony with the politics."

I tell him that I have heard that he is the only politician ever elected on an environmental platform in Louisiana, and he denies this adamantly enough to convince me that his political opponents would use such a label against him. "I'm a people-ist," he says. At first, I hear "populist," but he says it again: "People-ist."

"After a while," he says, "I realized that environmentalism and people-ism are synonymous." He won the Conservationist of the Year award from the Louisiana Wildlife Federation, he was named Rookie of the Year by the Louisiana Environmentalist Action Network, and he has been commended by the Louisiana Legislative Environment and Health Hall of Fame, but he does not want these things held against him. His political base extends beyond the environment. He won the Golden Award from the Terrebonne Parish NAACP, he won the Fred Henderson Award from the Louisiana Alliance for the Mentally Ill, and he was called a "Friend of Education" by the Louisiana Association of Educators. He fought tax breaks that exempted industry from school millages, he fought what he called "a stealth bill" that would have rendered state economic planning even more opaque than it already is, he supported a bill that would protect the crab meat industry from low-cost imports, he voted to make helmets mandatory apparel for motorcyclists, and he spoke against creation of a federally owned wildlife refuge that he saw as a waste of taxpayers' money. As part of a campaign advertisement, a checklist appeared that listed "Clean Environment" third, after "Good Schools" and "Safe Community."

"I always thought of myself as a conservative," he tells me, "but the pendulum just went too far. People are losing their rights. They're losing their access to the courts. It's frightening to me. My values didn't change, but I looked around and saw that conservative values had gone so far that the average person was getting screwed."

A little girl, dark haired and dark eyed, perhaps seven years old, comes into the kitchen. She is not Mike's daughter. From his comments, I understand her to be the daughter of a constituent. She looks down and around, shy in my presence because I am a stranger in this kitchen, but she does not hesitate in approaching Mike. He puts his hand on her back with affection, and she asks for a glass of water. I am immersed, unexpectedly, in a modern-day Norman Rockwell on-the-bayou, the relationship between a people-ist and a child too young to vote.

When the child leaves, Mike continues. "The people of Louisiana don't own this state," he says. "It's owned by foreign business. I don't mean foreign as in outside of the United States, but as in outside Louisiana. The profits are siphoned off. The industries don't have a vested interest in the state's long-term well-being. And industry runs the state. Big corporations don't believe in paying taxes, but they do believe in buying politicians, in controlling politicians. This is a democracy. I think the people should run the state, not industry. Whether its taxes or wetland restoration or whatever, I think the people should run the state."

He has been quoted calling a bill that provided tax exemptions to industry "corporate welfare, legalized robbery." He has, point blank, called industry representations lies. He has been quoted stating that Mike Foster, Louisiana's pro-industry governor, was against the "little people." Publicly, he has said that "putting a welder's helmet on the governor's head and calling him a common man is like putting a racing saddle on a jackass and calling it a thoroughbred."

Within Mike's district lies the community of Grand Bois, largely populated by Houma Indians. In 1994, a series of ten-truck convoys arrived in Grand Bois carrying industrial waste, officially classified, in the euphemistic world of Louisiana, as non-hazardous waste. Observers claim that convoy drivers en route to Grand Bois leapfrogged around one another—as a driver near the rear of the convoy felt the effects of fumes coming from the trucks ahead, he moved forward, to the front of the line, for fresh air.

At Grand Bois, at least one driver climbed down from the cab of his truck wearing rubber boots and a respirator. Meanwhile, children climbing out of school buses held shirts over their faces. A man with a video camera felt his skin burning and later developed a rash. A reporter allegedly ended her coverage of the situation in an emergency clinic.

Environmental Protection Agency director Carol Browner has commented on the kind of waste dumped in Grand Bois, claiming that the oil industry has a "sweetheart deal." In short, she explained that the dumping was legal, but the law was flawed. "You don't have to know what's in this waste," she said. "All you have to do is say, 'This waste came out of the ground when I sank an oil well.' And whatever comes out of the ground, you don't have to test it, you don't have to understand what's in it, you can dump it anywhere."[44] Under the law, what the trucks carried into Grand Bois was non-hazardous waste not because of what it was, but because of where it had come from. Samples from open pits in Grand Bois contain lead, benzene, toluene, xylene, sulfides—the stuff of Dante's nightmares. But dwellings stand within three hundred feet of the open pits. The entire community resides within one-half mile of the open pits. In samples from one of these pits, levels of benzene were thirty thousand times higher than the level required for classification as a hazardous waste under federal guidelines.

Mike has voters in Grand Bois, but his vision extends beyond that one community. He sees waste disposal in Louisiana as one more manifestation of big industry running the state. He talks of sweetheart deals between the state and the private sector with disgust. He does not believe that state-sanctioned enticements intended to bring industry to the state are good for his constituents. Companies get tax exemptions because they claim to bring jobs to the state, but he questions whether or not those jobs materialize. "Big business," he says, "influences with fear. We don't own our state."

He likes to compare industrial contamination in Louisiana with the history of lead regulation. In a report to the Department of Natural Resources Oil Field Waste Advisory Committee, he claims that the mining industry prevented regulation of lead long after its toxicity was well known. He quotes an Environmental Defense Fund paper claiming that the lead industry, in the years after World War I, controlled medical research, set public health priorities, and blocked the flow of anti-lead information.[45] He suggests that two renowned physicians, one from Harvard and the other from the Kettering Institute, were effectively bought out by industry. One of these physicians said that only a retarded child would eat paint and that any link between lead and retardation was coincidental. By the 1970s, it was recognized that lead poisoned more than ten thousand American children each year, leaving about two hundred dead and another five thousand retarded. Midway through Mike's report to the Department of Natural Resources Oil Field Waste Advisory Committee is a chilling sentence: "This author sees little difference between the actions of the lead industry and those of the Oil and Gas Industry."

While paddling on Bayou Trepanier, Mark Davis had suggested the need to look at contamination as a component of restoration. "They refuse to look closely at the situation," he had said. "They don't want to think about it. And if they don't think about it, they can't come to a rational decision." I ask Mike about the dichotomy separating contamination and restoration, if he believes that people are selling out, ignoring contamination at the request of industry.

"Resources can affect opinion," he says. "People are influenced by various things. Do you influence someone with money? Do you influence someone with women? Do you influence someone with ego? With fear? All of that's going on. Legislators are influenced by fear of big business. I don't know how all of these guys are influenced in every case. Money at times has been a factor. There's no question of that."

"Can scientists be influenced by money?" I ask.

"There's no question of that," he repeats. His chair squeaks again as he leans back. "You can buy any opinion you want. But it can be more subtle than that. The opinion influencers out there think about ways to influence people. They own newspapers. You can influence people by not reporting information. You can get inside peoples' heads without them ever knowing you were there."

"You said earlier that oil-field canals can account for about a third of the state's coastal wetland losses," I say. "But Gene Turner, at Louisiana

State University, says that the true effect of oil-field canals is much higher than that, closer to 99 percent of losses. Whether you agree with him or not, do you think that big oil in Louisiana has enough of a sweetheart deal to silence this idea even if it is true?"

"No question about that," he says for the third time, though he's quick to point out that others scientists do not agree with Gene's estimates.

I summarize Feyerabend's ideas about advocacy in science, telling Mike about Feyerabend's contention that objectivity is a pretense, that the reality is one in which scientists advocate their own ideas.

"I'm not familiar with Feyerabend," Mike says, "but I can understand the concept. As a politician, I come up with an idea, and even if something a little better comes along I may just want to stay in love with my own idea."

I take this concept further, suggesting that one way to influence scientists would be to reach them while their ideas are still coalescing, before they become advocates of a particular idea or position. In this way, a scientist could maintain integrity, but be influenced. A scientist's head could be accessed without the scientist ever realizing what has happened.

"Big picture," Mike says. "Big picture: The guys who influence opinion sit down together and brainstorm or sit down on their own and think, 'How do we best manipulate the data in this area?' or 'How do we best manipulate public opinion?' That's what I would do if I were them. I'd get some psychologists and I'd say, 'Look, we've got this guy Robichaux, and he reads a lot and he does this, that, and the other thing.' And they'd tell me, 'Okay, if you want to influence Robichaux you've got to go at him from this direction.' It may work and it may not. But you try to influence everyone. You try to reach as many people as you can. As long as it works some of the time, you've won. It's inconceivable to me that these people, people with that kind of money, do not do this."

"Can an agency scientist or a nontenured faculty scientist at LSU challenge the technical merit of a big restoration project?" I ask.

"Only with great difficulty," Mike answers. "By political design, scientists have to be subservient to political needs. I've seen it. Good people, good guys, people I felt very comfortable with, will give one answer in a group of five or six people and another answer publicly. Their futures depend on this." My impression is that he does not think these people are lying, but rather that their vision flexes under the spell of an instinctive survival mechanism without their realizing it.

Mike talks admiringly of James Eads, a nineteenth-century engineer who had fought federally funded navigation and flood control projects because they lacked technical merit. Eads eventually won some of his battles, but Eads was a man whose genius has been compared to that of Leonardo da Vinci and Thomas Edison.[46] And even for Eads, the battles had been won at an enormous cost: his personal relationships were strained, his health suffered, he faced bankruptcy more than once.

I tell Mike about *Michael X. St. Martin & Virginia Rayne St. Martin v. Mobil Exploration & Producing U.S., Inc., et al.,* in which technical information presented by wetland scientists was not, from the viewpoint of the judge, "very helpful."[47]

"I wonder," I say, "if that is a general perception about scientists? That they aren't very helpful, and that they can't agree on anything? Or that scientists are just one more lobbying group?"

"Politicians rely on scientists for expert information," he says. "But there are scientists, scientists, scientists. There are personal agendas. There are agency agendas."

Despite all of this, he believes that good research can go on in Louisiana. "There are scientists doing good work in Louisiana," he says. "Good, useful work."

He seems, in this matter, to agree with Sammy King: "The true grit," Sammy had said, "comes from reigning yourself in. If the data don't support your ideas, you need the strength to abandon the ideas." But, importantly, Mike thinks the time for action is here. He returns again to the pipeline concept and again points out that the time to cut bait has passed.

"We need this big project on the table," he says again. "A pipeline that delivers Mississippi River sediment down Bayou Lafourche, that's something that could be useful. It's not my idea. I can't take credit for it. But it's the scale of thinking we need. The sediment pipeline is a place to start. It may be wrong. There may be better ideas. There may be technical problems. But it's a starting point. Let's get it on the table even if we're just going to knock it off with some other idea." The technical problems include a need for booster pumps spaced every three or four miles along the pipe, the tendency for moving sediment to wear through pipeline walls in a matter of months, the possibility of permanently clogging a pipe if the flow stops even for a few minutes, and, above all else, the cost.

He pauses, then leans forward, elbows on the table, appearing suddenly tired. "People are talking about more development at Port Fourchon, near the end of Bayou Lafourche," he says. "But one good storm and the road to Port Fourchon is gone. It might take us a year to rebuild it. And Port Fourchon won't even be there fifty years from now if we don't do something soon."

Port Fourchon currently handles thirty million tons of cargo each year: steel pipe, barite, limestone, fuel. In some projections of land loss in Louisiana, Port Fourchon will be underwater by 2050.

Coming into Baton Rouge from the north, along the Mississippi River, the capitol stands against the sky, pale stone with a flag at its peak, the highest point in Louisiana. Behind the building, near the visitors' parking lot, willow trees and elephant ear surround Capitol Lake. A water control structure joins the lake to the Mississippi River. An egret stands in the shallows. A turtle's head breaks the surface, leaving behind circular ripples. But the skyline around the lake includes a massive refinery, a casino, and a construction site with two cranes. Mark Davis had called Bayou Trepanier a microcosm of Louisiana, but here, next to the capitol, is another microcosm, right under the noses of the state's legislators.

Inside the capitol, a laminated poster says, "Save Coastal Louisiana. Louisiana is losing thousands of acres of land each year!" Pictures of birds, an alligator, and children with fishing poles surround the words. The poster is attached to a case that holds a touch-screen computer with information about coastal Louisiana. I sit near the touch-screen display for twenty minutes, and more than a hundred people walk past, but the touch-screen remains untouched.

I make my way to Committee Room 5, then sit to wait for the joint

House and Senate Committee on Natural Resources meeting. The room resembles a theater, with 105 folding seats for the audience and a stage comprised of arched rows of desks—seating for the representatives and senators, each with a tall black microphone. The microphones stand like rows of storks across the front of the room.

The meeting is scheduled for 9:30. Representatives and senators, along with staffers, trickle in. One representative leaves when he discovers that there is no coffee. A senator sits and chats cheerfully about a new retirement bill under consideration. Another senator lectures to a young female staffer, explaining how the 1957 Sputnik launch raised ladies hemlines and lengthened their heels. Lobbyists also trickle in. Mark Davis shows up, wearing a dark suit and white shirt, shaking hands with fully half of the people in the room, all smiles even though some of these people undoubtedly see him as a major thorn in their sides. The meeting starts promptly at five minutes before ten.

Colonel Tom Julich, commander of the New Orleans District of the Corps of Engineers, sits at the front of the audience, at a desk facing the committee members. He wears his uniform, with various badges and insignias. A two-inch metal Corps Castle, the official emblem of the Corps of Engineers, is pinned to the lapel of his uniform. He is a West Point graduate with a master's degree in civil engineering. He now oversees a five-hundred-million-dollar annual budget, money used in coastal and central Louisiana. His jurisdiction covers six major and untold minor flood control structures, twelve navigation locks, twenty-eight hundred miles of navigable waterways, and just under a thousand miles of levees and flood walls. The combined length of Colonel Julich's navigable water-- ways, levees, and flood walls approaches the length of the Great Wall of China. In addition to all of this, in his spare time, he chairs the Federal-State CWPPRA Task Force, the group that manages thirty-five million dollars a year in restoration money. Sue Hawes, a Corps employee and board member on the Coalition to Restore Coastal Louisiana, and also a well-known expert on restoration in coastal Louisiana, sits to the colonel's right.

Colonel Julich reads from typewritten notes, but this is apparent only because I sit behind him and can see over his shoulder. He tells the committee about land losses in Louisiana, but also about gains. With the can-do attitude of a military background, he refers to Corps involvement in restoration as "doing what we need to do along our coast." He tells the committee about Corps dredging projects, which move, he says, enough material to fill fifteen superdomes every year. The material has been used to create eleven square miles of wetland since 1985. The numbers are impressive, and may be intended to impress, but they translate to the creation of wetlands, in fifteen years, equivalent in size to four months worth of wetland loss. The total CWPPRA package, he says, will preserve and restore 115,000 acres over the next fifty years, but Louisiana will still lose more than 400,000 acres. He tells the committee that the major restoration efforts in Louisiana "will address less than 10 percent of the marsh loss faced over the next half century."

Like almost everyone I have spoken to in the last eighteen months, Colonel Julich, too, realizes that Louisiana's bottom is falling out. He talks about the Coast 2050 plan, which strives to coordinate restoration efforts and to build a coherent strategy in the fight to save Louisiana. He reminds the committee that Louisiana needs to put funds into restoration if the federal government is to continue with its investment program. "Large-scale projects," he says, "call for large-scale dollars." He tells the committee that the federal government sets priorities based on state support—on the amount of money spent by the state and the outcomes of state activities. "Right now," he says, "the money is not there for Coast 2050." He throws out the price tag of fourteen billion dollars over thirty years.

Afterwards, Mike Robichaux compliments the colonel's presentation. But then he takes the opportunity to underscore the colonel's message of land loss, apparently trying to ensure that his committee colleagues understand the extent of the problem. From this, he moves to the sediment pipeline idea, placing it squarely on the table. "The 2050 plan is a giant step, but we need to take another giant step beyond that," he says. "I'd like to see us lay a pipeline from one of our sources of sediment and move this sediment down to some of our more endangered wetlands. We could use existing pipelines or whatever. I'd like to see us do something like this or just prove that it can't be done."

In response, Sue Hawes, sitting to the colonel's right, tells the committee that there are ownership problems with using existing pipelines and that sediment scours pipe walls and destroys the pipe. But when Mike suggests laying a dedicated pipeline down the center of Bayou Lafourche, a pipeline made to handle dredged sediment, Sue's response demonstrates her open mindedness: "It might work," she says.

Later, in a crowded elevator headed to the upper floors of the capitol, a woman wearing a staff badge and carrying a stack of folders talks to her companion. "It's been my experience," she says, "that nothing simple and sensible moves forward in Louisiana."

"What makes you think," her companion asks, "that Louisiana is so special?"

Lessons from Louisiana

I have, over the course of eighteen months, talked at length to more than forty people whose lives have become entangled with the fight to save Louisiana. I have had shorter conversations with another fifty. I have a list of at least a hundred others who could contribute to my understanding of what is happening in Louisiana. I have read over five thousand pages of technical reports, scientific papers, media releases, magazine articles, and memoranda. I have visited fifty-three restoration sites. But lasting impressions are as elusive as lasting marshes. Just as understanding starts to build, new ideas bury it or chip away at its edges. Comprehension subsides. Concepts erode.

Relevant vignettes come from many sources:

"There's an increasing awareness of just how much we don't know. The next five years will be very exciting, as we compare restored sites and reference sites. The public is beginning to see that this is not a simple issue. There is a lack of certainty."

"We don't understand cause and effect. There is pressure to move forward, to do something. People say, 'Let's do something, even if it's wrong.' I'd like to see more risk assessment up front, from both ecological and engineering viewpoints. But right now everyone wants to move and move fast."

"We've got a toehold on this problem. But that's all we've got is a toehold."

"I don't know my role outside of writing scientific papers. In my job, I'm promoted or not, based on scientific papers. But I want to be ready. If someone asks me about restoration, I'm here. And when that time comes I want to be clear if I'm talking about data or value judgements. I can say something important about data, about technical issues, but I have no more to say than anyone else if we're talking about a value judgement."

"We've got two camps: We're doing good, and we're doing bad. I'm starting a third camp: We're irrelevant. Sometimes I don't think we'll see any real progress for two hundred years."

"We're not anywhere close to perfect."

"I'm not a scientist, but I'm not stupid. I work on the ground, in the real world. Sometimes my hands get greasy. I just finished changing the oil in an airboat. When I talk to someone from the state, a kid with a master's degree who's trying to tell me what to do based on some science he learned in a classroom, I get frustrated. I want to tell him, 'Go manage ten thousand acres for a year and then come talk to me.' "

"As a scientist, I get the impression that people don't want to talk to me. They don't want to talk to me because they don't like what I have to say."

"As a manager, I see science as good and bad. Sometimes scientists want excessive study. Things that will work get slowed down."

"Scientists? Right now, they're doing a study of a study. I'm not joking. They're using tax dollars to study a study. We need money to get things done on the ground."

"Scientists have a tough problem. They want to think that it's all the same. But they know it's not all the same. So the politicians and the guys with the money go to the scientists and say, 'Tell us what to do.' But what the scientists know from one place just doesn't apply in another place."

"Scientists don't always know what they're talking about. Some science promotes deterioration of the land. Managing land out here in west Louisiana, we have to put up with ideas spilling over from the Deltaic Plain.

These ideas just don't apply out here. Sometimes we have to combat science."

"Sometimes science is ignored. Sometimes people prefer a seat-of-the-pants approach. I go to them as a scientist, and they say, 'What you're telling me may work where you are, but things are different here. We know how to do this.' Then their project fails."

"I manage 125,000 acres of coastal Louisiana. Do I use science in my management? I manage with tradition tainted by science or science tainted by tradition. I'm not sure which."

"Scientists as a lobbying group? That may be, but we're not a very effective lobbying group."

"Policy makers are hearing the scientists. At least, I hope they are. But what the scientists need to remember is that this is America. Everyone gets to vote."

"One man, one vote. My opinion as a scientist is no more valued than anyone else's. We spend our lives studying these systems, learning about these systems, but in the end, my input is no more valued than anyone else's. That's discouraging. But it's also democratic."

Curtis Richardson, director of the Duke Wetland Center in North Carolina, is known for his work in the Florida Everglades, the site of a restoration program comparable in scope and ambition to that occurring in Louisiana. "In the Everglades," he says, "people focus on individual pieces of the problem. There's a lack of resolve to look at the big picture. We're like the three blind men looking at an elephant—one man feels the trunk, one man feels the leg, and one man feels the body. But it's even worse than that. We're not even looking at the same elephant. Half the time we're not even looking at the same kind of animal."

Unquestionably, Louisiana strives to see the whole elephant. Greg Steyer, with Louisiana's Department of Natural Resources, believes that the state is a leader in the restoration arena. "We give lots of presentations on what we are learning," he tells me. "In the early nineties, our scale was so much greater than everyone else's that they couldn't pigeonhole us. But now large-scale approaches are attracting more attention. People want to hear what we have to say. One thing we did as part of our program design was to look at other projects. We looked at the Everglades, San Francisco Bay, Chesapeake Bay, and some EPA programs. We tried to look at all of the major restoration programs that were out there in order to see the different approaches. Most of what was going on was just planting—people planting wetland grasses or trees. Well, we don't do much planting in Louisiana. We do some planting, but really we need things here that go way beyond planting. And the majority of programs that we looked at didn't even have a monitoring requirement. There was almost no documentation of follow-up. At best, they might look at survival of plants for a couple of years. So we couldn't learn much from other projects. We're out on our own. We're guinea pigs for the nation when it comes to restoration and ecosystem management at this scale."

"Did Greg say guinea pigs for the nation?" someone asks me. "I'd say for the world—guinea pigs for the world."

Judge Edwards, a land manager named for a family member who was a judge, tells me that the big picture approach is the most promising thing he sees in Louisiana. "I'm living off of small projects," he tells me. "It's the small projects that make a difference on my land. But things are changing on the whole coast. We have the whole coast to save. We need to look at the big picture."

"We're under more pressure than they are in other states," says Bill Good, also with Louisiana's Department of Natural Resources. "We've got more at stake. The Delta is dying. People are affected directly. They can see the changes in their own lifetimes. They can see the impact on their communities, on their roads, their jobs. We're not talking about bugs and bunnies out here. We're talking about people, about a way of life. In other places, you might get away with looking at symptoms, but here you've got to look at the landscape. You've got to look at the landscape and the people. What's happening here in Louisiana is a good case study linking the environment and the economy. What happens here underscores what will happen anywhere that the environment is ignored. The environment drives the economy. It's pay me now or pay me later, not just here in Louisiana, but everywhere."

He wants to set the record straight. In a position of responsibility, in a position of authority, Bill Good once publicly stated that CWPPRA was not about science. "I was never anti-research," he tells me. "I'm a scientist myself. Both of my parents were scientists. We've learned a lot from scientists. People like Don Cahoon, Robert Twilley, Denise Reed, Andy Nyman, Irv Mendelssohn. . . . It's a big list. But in the early days, too much money was spent on research. The money was meant for restoration, not for science, not for keeping university scientists employed. I might have over-reacted at one time, trying to get restoration back on track by distancing CWPPRA from research funding. But that overreaction may have been necessary. Now we have a good balance. Science is at the core of our work."

"In other places," he says, "all their energy goes into litigation. We have some litigation here, but not much. Our energy goes to restoration. And when it comes to technology versus social, we're way ahead in the technology department. I'll give you an example. What do you do when a restoration project shifts natural resources? What happens if a restoration project increases oyster production over a hundred square miles, but hurts it in a two-square-mile patch? Someone was harvesting oysters off that two-square-mile patch, and your restoration project just put them out of business. The genius of CWPPRA is that it forces us to work together. Under CWPPRA, the public is involved with everything we do, with the entire decision-making process. We have to consult with everyone who might be impacted by our projects, so we have every interest group you can imagine involved. In this setting, the process is just as important as the end product. If we don't have this process of public involvement, no one will be satisfied with the product, no matter how good it is. People have to participate to be satisfied. And we have to balance people and science."

Beth Middleton, who teaches restoration principles to college students in Illinois, talks about restoration in her part of the country. "From the outset, people don't see the landscape. But the landscape around the project influences the project. Scientists have a duty to talk about how it really is rather than the way people would like it to be. They may not make friends, but they have to do this. You may feel like they're ganging up on you. Stepping in front of the power players is a sure way to get run down.

But we have to say what we have to say. What good are we if we don't do this?"

In Louisiana, scientists are seeing the landscape. They are talking about how it really is. They are not necessarily making friends, even among themselves. For almost every idea that I have uncovered over the past year, someone out there is ready to disagree. More often then not, a statement disagreeing with someone's idea is likely to begin as follows: "I like him, but . . ." Occasionally, the statement begins with "I like him" and deteriorates toward swearing before the sentence ends. Sometimes the "I like him" is dispensed with altogether, and the statement starts and ends with swearing. Although I write "him" as though women are exempt, they are not.

I say that Louisiana scientists are seeing the landscape, but there remains a matter of scale. Bill Mitsch, a professor with Ohio State University who sometimes describes himself as "thinking out of the box," talks about combating the dead zone problem by converting 3 percent of the farmland in the Mississippi River's drainage into wetlands. That 3 percent could not remove all of the agricultural chemicals that cause the dead zone, but it could make what he casually refers to as "a substantial dent." "Of course it's the whole basin that should be fixed," he says. "They should be going upstream, too, away from the coast. They shouldn't just focus on the coast."

Joy Zedler, the Aldo Leopold Chair of Restoration at the University of Wisconsin and one of the world's leading voices in the science of restoration, says that scientists are better able than managers to step back from a situation, to see the bigger picture. "Scientists," she says, "link theory and context."

When I ask her if restoration projects draw from the best available information, if they incorporate the best available science into design and construction, she is quick to answer: "No," she says simply. When I pursue the matter further, she tells me that, in her experience, restoration managers tend to rely on anecdotal information, things they have heard from their immediate professional circles, things limited to a local context. But she has never worked in Louisiana. In Louisiana, restoration managers are moving beyond anecdotal information. It is, as I had been told, tradition tainted by science or science tainted by tradition.

In Louisiana, the depth of feeling about wetlands cannot be overstated. "Every acre lost in Louisiana, I'm a part of it," says a land manager in Vermilion Parish.

"These marshes are my life," says a fisherman in Plaquemines Parish.

On the other hand, there is this comment about public involvement from a land manager in south Louisiana: "You have to go to every meeting, every meeting, every meeting. If you miss one meeting, your project is history. Guys who don't go don't get." And I think of Mike Robichaux telling me that, if he had the time, he would be jumping up and down to endorse his sediment pipeline, but that his responsibilities are divided between many issues. His project, his vision of using a proven technology to move sediment to the end of Bayou Lafourche, subsides under the weight of other projects. "Guys who don't go don't get."

Curtis Richardson, speaking again about restoration in the Florida Everglades, talks about project failures. "There can be a loss of objectivity post construction. We may look at three projects and say, 'Okay, one of these will work.' We chose one and build it. To build it, it has to be sold as a fix, not as an experiment. But every restoration should be seen as an experiment. After spending millions of tax dollars, it's hard to say something is a failure. It is not that anyone lies about what's happening or fudges data. It is a matter of omission. We just don't look closely at what we've done." Within some quarters of Louisiana's scientific community, a similar perception exists, a perception that the powers that be—the agencies responsible for large-scale restoration in Louisiana—are unwilling to admit failure.

This does not seem to be true, as these vignettes illustrate:

"CWPPRA can admit failure. A couple of projects have been deauthorized. Outside of Louisiana, no one reports failures. They don't even look. Sometimes to get a project going, you've got to promise the moon. Outside of Louisiana what I see is people promising the moon and then looking away. Here in Louisiana, we look at our projects."

"The public feels that projects should be successful. They don't recognize that restoration is a new science, that what we're implementing here is truly experimental. In our work, in our reports, we recognize this. But the public doesn't understand it."

"Every project is monitored for twenty years, and all of the monitoring is linked to project goals."

"We're going to go up some blind alleys. We make the rules as we go. That's what we have to do. No one has been this way before, so that's what we have to do. We're going to learn some things the hard way."

"When we see that a project isn't working, we try to take the next step and make it work. If we're not meeting our goals, we can tweak the project and improve it."

"The public doesn't understand that this is experimental. Some members of the public get into this hip deep, but most don't. Most have an emotional response—fear, anxiety, frustration. They say, 'Why can't you fix it? Why is it so expensive? Why is it taking so long?' They feel like they know what to do. 'Just do this,' they might say, or, 'This is what my grandfather says needs to be done, and he was here before it started to disappear.' They get frustrated because we look too cautious. They think we over-intellectualize the problem. They think we're ignoring failures. But we're not ignoring anything."

Several people point to the terraces in Calcasieu Lake, where I had sampled fish with Lawrence Rozas, as a failure. They tell me that the terrace cells were supposed to fill with sediment and build marsh, but that they have not. I ask Greg Steyer at Louisiana's Department of Natural Resources about the terracing project.

"The concept for terracing came from the Netherlands," he says. "We tried to sell that project in a lot of ways: breaking up wave energy, encouraging aquatic plants, trapping sediments. We had nine goals. We tried to measure sediment accumulation with marker horizons, but the feldspar didn't last. Remember, this was nine years ago, before Sediment Elevation Tables were in vogue, so we didn't have any Sediment Elevation Tables out there. Remember, too, that there isn't much sediment in the water in Calcasieu Lake. So maybe it didn't fill in, so it didn't meet the sediment-trapping goal, at least to the extent of building marsh. But it did meet some of its other goals, so it was not a failure. And we learned from it. We've put in more terraces since then. The Little Vermilion Bay terraces did not have sediment trapping as a goal."

I ask Bill Good for specific examples of failed projects. "We used Christmas trees to protect shorelines from erosion," he says, "but that didn't work. They just broke up. And we pumped some sediment onto Raccoon Island, but the sediment was too fine. It wouldn't stack up. That happened at another site, too. A marsh management project in Terrebonne Parish didn't work out like we had hoped."

Joy Zedler, from her office in Wisconsin, talks about failure and success. "We're rarely interested in admitting failure," she says. "There's a problem with the words 'failure' and 'success.' The whole problem with the word 'success' is that if you have success you have to have failure. And no one wants to say the word 'failure.' They'll say 'partial success' or 'incomplete success' but they won't say 'failure.' And they're right. Almost no project is a complete failure. A project may not do everything we want it to do, but it does some things."

"We make progress," a land manager tells me, "but it's hard going. It's a chore." And I remember Sammy King summarizing his optimism about restoration: "It's a slow process, but we're moving forward," he had said.

One task remains. I drive again to the Old River Control Structure. I pass the Sidney A. Murray Jr. Hydroelectric Station, I pass the Low Sill Structure, and I pass the Auxiliary Control Structure. I cross over the lock and canal, the navigation artery joining the Atchafalaya and Mississippi Rivers, and park near where I had met the man who had shown me the workings of the Old River Control Structure. He had told me, among other things, that I would find wetland experts behind every tree. That had proven to be an exaggeration. Behind every second tree would have been closer to the mark.

From the top of my jeep, I pull down my sea kayak, a handmade product from my own basement, an odd craft for the Atchafalaya River, a stretched out and round-bottomed pirogue. I launch from the boat ramp and paddle along the canal leading away from the locks and toward the main flow of the Atchafalaya River. A family fishes from the bank—the father shirtless, the son listlessly throwing stones into the water, and the mother sitting under the shade of a beach umbrella. It is something more than a mile between the boat ramp and the end of the canal, where the canal joins Old River. Where they join, a long stretch of floating dredge pipe has been stored along the northern bank. It is four more miles between Old River and the Atchafalaya River. By kayak, moving downstream, the trip from the boat ramp to the Atchafalaya River requires just over an hour of paddling. I share the channel with bass boats, a small sailing yacht, and a petroleum barge flying the flag of Texas as it moves toward the locks. Along the banks, sycamore and willow trees stand in several feet of water. Songbirds call from the foliage. A pair of grain barges and eight barges loaded with stone are moored near shore. Schools of mullet churn the surface with their snouts and a gar swims sharklike, with its dorsal fin out of the water.

I join the Atchafalaya River and follow the current. Paddling on top of sediment from Ohio, Arkansas, North Dakota, Tennessee, I move toward the newest delta lobe of the Mississippi River. I am about eighty miles south of Sammy King's research sites in the Tensas National Wildlife Refuge and perhaps fifty miles from Norman Haigh's land. In the other direction, it is two hundred miles to Don Cahoon's sites at North Grants Pond and, catty-corner to that, two hundred miles to Lawrence Rozas's fish traps in Calcasieu Lake.

It is July, at eleven in the morning. The humidity and temperature both hover around ninety. In the middle of the river, the only shade is under the kayak. Sweat mixed with sunscreen burns my eyes. In this heat, the river becomes a metaphor for what I have seen over the past eighteen months: Particles moving down the river are like ideas, all heading in the same general direction, but with no clear future. Some will sink in deep water. Some will flow into the Gulf and follow the mudstream to the Chenier Plain. Some will become part of the Atchafalaya Delta. It is impossible to know which will be which. All of them are part of this land-building process. One clear message, the unanimous message, is that opening the Old River Control Structure, letting the Atchafalaya capture the Mississippi, is foolishness—far more foolish than, say, running a pipeline down the middle of Bayou Lafourche, pumping sand to rebuild barrier islands, diverting the Mississippi River's water and sediment, or backfilling canals. In a landscape of people, the Old River Control Structure becomes nothing less than good business.

I move downstream from the confluence of Old River and the Atchafalaya River, toward the Atchafalaya Delta, for thirty minutes. Today, for most people, is a workday. Somewhere in Louisiana people debate the pros and cons of a particular approach to restoration. People look at data. People try to figure out the next step forward. Strength grows from diversity.

It is time to head back toward the boat ramp. I stop paddling long enough to drink a bottle of water. As I drink, my kayak turns. Briefly, I am sideways to the current, then I am facing upstream, and then downstream again, having come full circle as I flow toward the Gulf. The kayak spins in the current while I finish drinking, then I paddle upstream. The current, one-third of the Mississippi River's flow working against me, is strong. I make progress, but it is a chore.

NOTES

1. R. G. Kazmann and D. B. Johnson, "If the Old River Control Structure Fails? (The Physical and Economic Consequences)," *Louisiana Water Resources Research Institute Bulletin* 12 (Baton Rouge: Louisiana State University, 1980).

2. U.S. Army Corps of Engineers, *Atchafalaya Outlet, Mississippi River and Tributaries,* brochure, U.S. Army Engineer District, New Orleans, LA, 1981.

3. U.S. Army Corps of Engineers, *Old River Control,* New Orleans District U.S. Army Corps of Engineers, New Orleans, LA, 1993.

4. J. G. Gosselink, "The Ecology of Delta Marshes of Coastal Louisiana: A Community Profile," U.S. Fish and Wildlife Service, FWS/OBS-84/09, U.S. Department of the Interior, Washington, DC, 1984; C. R. Kolb and J. R. Van Lopik, "Geology of the Mississippi Deltaic Plain—Southeastern Louisiana." Waterways Experiment Station Technical Report 2: 3–482, Vicksburg, MS, 1958; R. T. Saucier, "Geomorphology and Quarternary Geologic History of the Lower Mississippi Valley," Waterways Experiment Station, Vicksburg, MS, 1994.

5. Kazmann and Johnson, "If the Old River Control Structure Fails?" 9.

6. R. E. Turner and N. N. Rabalais, "Coastal Eutrophication near the Mississippi River Delta," *Nature* 368 (1994): 619–21.

7. R. E. Turner, "Wetland Loss in the Northern Gulf of Mexico: Multiple Working Hypotheses," *Estuaries* 20 (1997): 1–13.

8. H. L. Steward, "Off-base about Wetlands Loss," *Times-Picayune,* June 8, 1997.

9. Turner, "Wetland Loss in the Northern Gulf of Mexico: Multiple Working Hypotheses."

10. P. Feyerabend, *Against Method* (New York: Verso Books, 1993).

NOTES

11. J. V. Letter, "Wetland Engineering in Coastal Louisiana: Mississippi River Delta Splays," WRP Technical Note WG-RS-7.1, Waterways Experiment Station, Vicksburg, MS, 1997.

12. M. Boyer, J. Harris, and R. E. Turner, "Constructed Crevasses and Land Gain in the Mississippi River Delta," *Journal of Restoration Ecology* 5 (1997): 85–92.

13. R. E. Turner and M. E. Boyer, "Mississippi River Diversions, Coastal Wetland Restoration/Creation and an Economy of Scale," *Ecological Engineering* 8 (1997): 117–28.

14. R. E. Turner, E. M. Swenson, and J. M. Lee, "A Rationale for Coastal Wetland Restoration through Spoil Bank Management in Louisiana, U.S.A.," *Environmental Management* 18 (1994): 271–82.

15. C. Neill and R. E. Turner, "Backfilling Canals to Mitigate Wetland Dredging in Louisiana Coastal Marshes," *Environmental Management* 11 (1987): 823–36.

16. N. B. Hobbs, "Mire Morphology and the Properties and Behavior of Some British and Foreign Peats," *Quarterly Journal of Engineering Geology* (London) 19 (1986):7–80.

17. W. H. Patrick, R. P. Gambrell, and S. P. Faulkner, "Redox Measurements of Soils," in *Methods of Soil Analysis,* part 3, "Chemical Methods," Soil Science Society of America Book Series, no. 5. (Madison, WI: Soil Science Society of America and American Society of Agronomy, 1996), 1255–73; S. P. Faulkner, R. P. Gambrell, and S. L. Ashby, "Analytical Methods for Iron and Manganese Determinations in Reservoir Tailwaters: Laboratory Investigations," Water Quality Technical Note PD-01, Waterways Experiment Station, Vicksburg, MS, 1996; S. P. Faulkner and W. H. Patrick, "Redox Processes and Diagnostic Wetland Soil Indicators in Bottomland Hardwood Forests," *Soil Science Society of America Journal* 56 (1992): 856–65.

18. M. E. Poach and S. P. Faulkner, "Soil Phosphorus Characteristics of Created and Natural Wetlands in the Atchafalaya Delta, LA," *Estuarine, Coastal and Shelf Science* 46 (1998): 195–203.

19. E. W. Garbisch, "Recent and Planned Marsh Establishment Work throughout the Contiguous United States, a Survey and Basic Guidelines," Waterways Experiment Station Report D-77-3, Waterways Experiment Station, Vicksburg, MS, 1977.

20. M. C. Landin, J. W. Webb, and P. L. Knudson, "Long-Term Monitoring of Eleven Corps of Engineers Habitat Development Field Sites Built of Dredged Material, 1974–1987," Waterways Experiment Station Technical Report D-89-1, Waterways Experiment Station, Vicksburg, MS, 1989; W. J. Streever, "*Spartina alterniflora* Marshes on Dredged Material: A Critical Review of the Ongoing Debate over Success," *Wetlands Ecology and Management* 8 (2000): 295–316.

21. P. Shea, K. A. Westphal, Q. Tao, C. Zganjar, P. Connor, J. Phillippe, L. Mathies, B. Nord, and J. Flanagan, "Beneficial Use of Dredged Material Monitoring Program,"

NOTES

1996 annual report, part 9, "Results of Monitoring the Beneficial Use of Dredged Material at the Atchafalaya River and Bayous Chene, Boeuf, and Black, Louisiana— Atchafalaya Bay/Delta and Bar Channel," U.S. Army Corps of Engineers, New Orleans District, New Orleans, LA, 1997.

22. D. J. Reed and D. R. Cahoon, "Marsh Submergence versus Marsh Accretion: Interpreting Accretion Deficit Data in Coastal Louisiana," in *Coastal Zone '93: Proceedings of the Eighth Symposium on Coastal and Ocean Management, July 19–23, 1993, New Orleans, Louisiana* (New York: American Society of Civil Engineers, 1993), 243–57; D. R. Cahoon and D. J. Reed, "Relationships among Marsh Surface Topography, Hydroperiod, and Soil Accretion in a Deteriorating Louisiana Salt Marsh," *Journal of Coastal Research* 11 (1995): 357–69; D. R. Cahoon, D. J. Reed, and J. W. Day, "Estimating Shallow Subsidence in Microtidal Salt Marshes of the Southeastern United States: Kaye and Barghoorn Revisited," *Marine Geology* 128 (1995): 1–9.

23. W. S. Perret, J. E. Roussel, J. F. Burdon, and J. F. Pollard, "Long-Term Trends of Some Trawl-Caught Estuarine Species in Louisiana," in *Coastal Zone '93: Proceedings of the Eighth Symposium on Coastal and Ocean Management, July 19–23, 1993, New Orleans, Louisiana* (New York: American Society of Civil Engineers, 1993), 3459–73.

24. Louisiana Coastal Wetlands Conservation and Restoration Task Force and the Wetlands Conservation and Restoration Authority, *Coast 2050: Toward a Sustainable Coastal Louisiana* (Baton Rouge: Louisiana Department of Natural Resources, 1998).

25. J. A. Browder, L. N. May, A. Rosenthal, J. G. Gosselink, and R. H. Baumann, "Modeling Future Trends in Wetland Loss and Brown Shrimp Production in Louisiana Using Thematic Mapper Imagery," *Remote Sensing of Environment* 28 (1989): 45–59.

26. T. J. Minello, R. J. Zimmerman, and R. Medina, "The Importance of Edge for Natant Macrofauna in a Created Salt Marsh," *Wetlands* 14 (1994): 184–98; G. W. Peterson and R. E. Turner, "The Value of Salt Marsh Edge vs Interior as a Habitat for Fish and Decapod Crustaceans in a Louisiana Tidal Marsh," *Estuaries* 17 (1994): 235–62; L. P. Rozas and D. J. Reed, "Nekton Use of Marsh-Surface Habitats in Louisiana (USA) Deltaic Salt Marshes Undergoing Submergence," *Marine Ecology Progress Series* 96 (1993): 147–57.

27. G. P. Kemp, "Mud Deposition at the Shoreface: Wave and Sediment Dynamics on the Chenier Plain of Louisiana" (Ph.D. diss., Louisiana State University, Baton Rouge, 1986).

28. Turner, "Wetland Loss in the Northern Gulf of Mexico: Multiple Working Hypotheses."

29. The Coalition to Restore Coastal Louisiana, *No Time to Lose: Facing the Future of Louisiana and the Crises of Coastal Land Loss* (Baton Rouge: Coalition to Restore Coastal Louisiana, 1999).

30. "Flood Rates Are on the Rise: Louisiana to Pay More for Insurance," *Times Picayune*, January 6, 1997, B-1.

31. "Insurers Wary of Homes in Louisiana," *Times Picayune*, January 11, 1997, Real Estate section, 1, 12–13.

32. S. L. King and B. D. Keeland, "Evaluation of Reforestation in the Lower Mississippi River Alluvial Valley," *Restoration Ecology* 7 (1999): 348–59.

33. S. L. King, "Bottomland Hardwood Forests: Past, Present, and Future," in *Ecology and Management of Bottomland Hardwood Systems: The State of Our Understanding*, ed. L. H. Fredrickson, R. M. Kaminski, and S. L. King (forthcoming).

34. G. R. Guntenspergen and B. A. Vairin, *Willful Winds: Hurricane Andrew and Louisiana's Coast* (Lafayette, LA: National Biological Service, 1996).

35. D. R. Cahoon, D. J. Reed, J. W. Day, G. D. Steyer, R. M. Boumans, J. C. Lynch, D. McNally, and N. Latif, "The Influence of Hurricane Andrew on Sediment Distribution in Louisiana Coastal Marshes," *Journal of Coastal Research* 21 (1995): 280–94.

36. L. P. Rozas and D. J. Reed, "Nekton Use of Marsh-Surface Habitats in Louisiana (USA) Deltaic Salt Marshes Undergoing Submergence," *Marine Ecology Progress Series* 96 (1993): 147–57.

37. U.S. Army Corps of Engineers, New Orleans District, Freshwater Diversions, undated booklet, U.S. Army Corps of Engineers, New Orleans District, New Orleans, LA.

38. D. J. Reed, "Patterns of Sediment Deposition in Subsiding Coastal Salt Marshes, Terrebonne Bay, Louisiana: The Role of Winter Storms," Estuaries 12 (1989): 222–27; D. J. Reed, "The Response of Coastal Marshes to Sea-Level Rise: Survival or Submergence?" *Earth Surface Processes and Landforms* 20 (1995): 39–48; D. J. Reed and A. L. Foote, "Effect of Hydrologic Management on Marsh Surface Sediment Deposition in Coastal Louisiana," *Estuaries* 20 (1997): 301–11.

39. Reed and Foote, "Effect of Hydrologic Management on Marsh Surface Sediment Deposition in Coastal Louisiana."

40. D. R. Cahoon and C. G. Groat, eds., A Study of Marsh Management Practice in Coastal Louisiana, vol. 2, Technical Description, OCS Study MMS 90-0076 (New Orleans, LA: U.S. Department of the Interior, 1990).

41. N. L. Kuhn, I. A. Mendelssohn, and D. J. Reed, "Altered Hydrology Effects on Louisiana Salt Marsh Function," *Wetlands* 19 (1999): 617–26.

42. Michael X. St. Martin & Virginia Rayne St. Martin v. Mobil Exploration & Producing U.S., Inc., et al., U.S. District Court, Eastern District of Louisiana, Civil Action no. 95-4128, sec. E/2, filed August 12, 1998.

43. Roman Catholic Church v. Louisiana Gas Service Co., 618 So. 2d 874, 879-880 (La. 1993).

44. M. Robichaux, "Report of State Senator Mike Robichaux to the State Committee on Oilfield Waste—September 1998," <http://senate.legis.state.la.us./Robichaux/Topics.asp>.

45. P. Reich, The Hour of Lead: A Brief History of Lead Poisoning in the United States over the Past Century and of Efforts by the Lead Industry to Delay Regulation (Washington, DC: Environmental Defense Fund, 1992).

46. J. Barry, *Rising Tide: The Great Mississippi Flood of 1927 and How It Changed America* (New York: Simon and Schuster, 1997).

47. Michael X. St. Martin & Virginia Rayne St. Martin v. Mobil Exploration & Producing U.S., Inc., et al.

INDEX

Accretion, 66–68, 73, 137, 142
Advocacy, in science, 23
Atchafalaya Delta, 37, 44, 46–47; flood of 1973, 48, 53; and wetland gain in, 49
Auxiliary Control Structure, 6, 12

Barataria Bay, 27, 88, 144
Barrier island restoration, 157
Beavers, 119
Belowground processes, 53, 82
Bird's Foot Delta, 3, 10, 28–30, 44, 69, 79, 88
Bonnet Carre Spillway, 14, 80, 110, 114, 138
Brants Pass, 78–79, 81
Breaux Bill, 34
Breaux's Cut, 52

Caernarvon, 103, 138, 144, 147–50, 159
Calcasieu Lake, 42, 83–99, 150, 177
Canals: backfilled, 25, 36–38, 40–41; wetland loss and, 19–20, 22, 25, 28, 75, 102

Channel Armor Gap, 81
Chenier Plain, 39–40, 91–92
Christmas trees, 178
Coalition to Restore Coastal Louisiana, 100, 104, 138, 145
Coast 2050, 74, 168
Coastal biogeomorphology, 137
Conservation Reserve Program, 116–17
Costs, of restoration, 35–36, 40, 84, 124
Crevasse, 31–32, 35, 69, 73, 145
Crevasse splay, 32, 36, 41, 44, 70
Cubit's Gap, 29–30
CWPPRA (Coastal Wetland Protection, Planning, and Restoration Act), 34–36, 40, 74, 80–81, 102, 113, 115, 117, 124, 142, 157–58, 167–68, 174

Davis Pond, 103, 138, 159
Dead zone, 19, 24, 45, 54, 129, 138, 175
Decomposition, 54–55
Delta farms, 26–27, 157
Delta National Wildlife Refuge, 29, 31–32, 52, 79–80

Deltaic Plain, 39–40
Deposition, 67, 73, 140
Dredged material wetlands, 35, 46–63, 114, 158
Dredging, 13, 49, 104, 110–12, 168

Eads, James, 165
Einstein, Hans, 11
Erosion, 10
Estuarine Research Federation, 108–09, 143

FEMA, 105
Feyerabend, Paul, 22–23, 43, 75, 103, 131, 164
Flood Control Act, 148
Freshwater diversions, 24, 138, 150, 159

Grants Pond, 69
Great Flood of 1927, 14

Hurricane Andrew, 134–35

Impoundments: restoration of, 27, 36; wetland loss and, 26
Intracoastal Waterway, 37

LaBranche, Bayou, 111, 114
Lafourche Delta, 10–11
Lake Pontchartrain Basin Foundation, 80
Landscape chemistry, 56
Lateral compression, 135
Lead toxicity, 162–63
Louisiana Department of Wildlife and Fisheries, 88
Louisiana Universities Marine Consortium (LUMCON), 134–35
Louisiana Water Resources Institute, 14
Low Sill Structure, 5–6, 8, 12

Lower Mississippi Alluvial Valley, 116, 120

Marker horizons, 54, 61, 66–67, 71–72, 78, 177
Market failure, 106–07
Marsh edge, 89–90, 96
Marsh management, 140, 143
Mississippi River Commission, 11
Morganza Floodway, 14
Mudstream, 91

National Marine Fisheries Service, 84, 90
National Wetlands Research Center, 64, 121
Native Americans: Grand Bois and, 161; Houma Indians and, 161; Mississippian Cultural Period and, 127; Woodland Cultural Period and, 126
New Madrid earthquakes, 131
No Time to Lose, 103–04, 106
North Grants Pond, 69–70, 73, 75, 79
Nuisance law, 108
Nuttall, Thomas, 131

Old River Control Project, 11
Old River Control Structure, 3, 178; Caernarvon and, 147; hubris and, 16; mudstream and, 91; near failure of, 4, 12, 48; opening of, 44–45, 79, 103, 144; wetland loss and, 8

Paradigm shifts, 22–23, 56, 121, 146
Planting, 35, 50, 118–19, 125, 127, 173
Project Flood, 13
Property values, 104
Pulsing paradigm, 145

Raccoon Island, 134
Regulatory failure, 106
Restore America's Estuaries, 108–09

Sabine National Wildlife Refuge, 42

Saint Bernard Delta, 9, 11, 22, 91

Salinization, 148

Sediment accumulation, 45, 62

Sediment Elevation Table (SET), 64, 68, 70–74, 79–81, 177

Sediment starvation, 20

Sediment traps, 141

Shreve's Cutoff, 9–10

Sidney A. Murray Hydroelectric Station, 13

Siphons, 35, 158

Splays, 29–30

Spoil banks, 26, 44

Spoil-bank management, 36, 43

Subdelta lobes, 29

Subsidence, 66–67, 73, 75; accretion and, 68, 142; dead trees and, 151; deep, 71; definition of, 10; Delta National Wildlife Refuge and, 79; law suit and, 152–53; marsh edge and, 89; plant growth and, 10, 73; speed of, 157

Surveying, 65

Swamp Land Acts, 26

Tensas National Wildlife Refuge, 121–30

Terraces, 35–36, 42, 83–99, 149, 177–78

Trepanier, Bayou, 106–14

Turnbull's Bend, 8

Valuation, 132

Volumetric leverage, 44, 62

Water Resources Development Act, 148

Wax Lake, 37

West Atchafalaya Floodway, 14

Wetland gain, 48

Wetland loss rates, 22

Wetland Value Assessment Method, 36

Wetlands Reserve Program, 116–17, 119–20

Whiskey Island, 134